A SPIRITUAL DUOLOGY ~ 2

Spiritual Reflections

Why are we alive?

Discover what awakening, enlightenment & spirituality are in this 2-book series of thoughtful, easily understandable spiritual reflections about life

Book 2

A SPIRITUAL BOOK BY

Ken Luball

Author's Note

"Why are we alive?" This timeless question lies at the heart of *'Spiritual Reflections' – Book 2*. Written in clear, easily understandable language, these 250 free verse poems use metaphor, imagery, and spiritual insight to explore themes of awakening, enlightenment, and the human pursuit of meaning, as it guides readers toward a deeper understanding of life's true purpose. To truly understand each reflection, read only two or three a day and reflect on each one.

My hope writing *'Spiritual Reflections'* was to try to awaken and help others who are awakened more fully understand what enlightenment is so their journey through life may be more fully realized.

As you prepare to begin your search for meaning, do so with an open heart and mind, ready to delve deeper into the mysteries of existence. Let us embark on this spiritual adventure together, and, in doing so, discover the answers you are searching for.

Glossary

Asleep – After we are born we are taught how to survive in the world and what success is. We therefore learn to worry only about our own success and survival in the world, rather than to be concerned about others. This results in living in a self-centered world of prejudice, inequity, and endless struggle. Those who fully believe this are asleep, accepting the status quo as the truth.

Awaken – There may come a time in our life when, despite our success in the world, we begin to question the truth of our self-centered learned beliefs, our ego. When this happens the first quiet messages of the spirit, a piece of god present within every life are sensed, beginning us on an enduring journey to discover meaning in our life.

Ego – The ego is everything we learn, believe, and accept is true after we are born, as we learn how to survive in a self-centered world. Its primary concern is what is best for us; it worries little about others. It also attempts to build up our self-esteem by convincing us of our value in the world.

Enlightenment – The complete acceptance of the spiritual path, allowing the spirit's inherent wisdom and unconditional love to be our primary guide in life. With enlightenment, the ego, our self-centered learned beliefs, assumes a secondary role in our life, no longer influencing the direction of our life choices.

Spirit/ Soul/ God / Higher-Self – An ethereal entity accompanying and inextricably connecting every life to another's. Its purpose is to give our lives meaning by sharing its inherent wisdom and unconditional love to help guide our life's choices.

Spirituality – Spirituality is the belief there is a piece of god, a spirit or soul within every life intimately linking each of us to the other, and, because of this, each life, regardless of our differences, accomplishments, or genus, is important, equal, and connected.

You Are Worthwhile

Though you may be
poor, struggle daily to
survive, your life is as
important as any other
that has achieved success
in the world.

Our body is but a shell,
housing our spirit within.
Our mind is but a tool
to accept society's beliefs.

Who we truly are, lies
not in our success or
thoughts, but in our
essence within.

The First Step to Awakening

Before beginning on a
spiritual path, we must
first start to question
our beliefs and attitudes
about the world.
We are brought up
to believe in always
putting our own needs
and desires before others.
To begin the awakening
process, this belief
must be reversed.

When we are able to
sincerely put the needs
of others, before only
considering our own desires,
treat all, without exception,
as equal, their lives
important, significant,
then we will have awoken,
beginning an enduring
journey to understand
our life's true purpose.

This is Enlightenment

Every life, regardless
of our differences or
genus, has a spirit, a
piece of god within,
intimately connecting
each to the other.
No one person or lifeform,
therefore, regardless of their
appearance, beliefs, or
accomplishments in life,
each with a piece of god
within is, or ever has been
better, their life more
important than another's.

Understanding this, then
selflessly sharing our
spirit's innate wisdom
and unconditional love
to help others realize this
as well, is enlightenment.

Reviewing My Life

I am in the twilight of life;
death will come soon.
I have no fear, though as I
look back over my life, there
are many things I wish
I had done differently.

Instead of worrying only
about myself and success in
the world, constantly working,
striving to enjoy life, I would
have spent more time helping
others and with those I love.
I would have listened, learned,
and assisted all those in need,
even strangers I did not know.
I would have fought harder to
change the world, feed the hungry,
provide shelter to the homeless,
and stop the prejudice, hate, and
senseless slaughter humanity
needlessly inflicts on each other.

I only wish I had understood
these things earlier, so my life
could have been more meaningful,
rather than simply being focused
on only what was best for myself.

Taking Advantage of Others

There is never a reason to do,
say, or imply harm to another.
It matters not if the slight
is verbal, physical, or
in any other manner.
We are all in life's journey together.
Though many believe the injury
they caused to the other is
trivial, in reality, it harms both.

Apart, regardless of our
success or accomplishments
in life, our lives are insignificant.
Only together, by always
helping others and treating
all with respect and
unconditional love, will
life's genuine meaning
become apparent.

Light

Light exists within each life.
It often is hidden from view
by our dominant self-centered
beliefs, our ego, quieting its
wisdom and dimming its
light from our life.

The intention of life is to
rediscover and then shine
our light on all others so
they too may find their
light within as well.

Remember

We are spirit, co-existing
in a corporeal body.
We forget this after we are
exposed to life's challenges.

Our life's purpose is to
remember, then selflessly
share our spirit's inherent
wisdom and unconditional
love to help others remember
their true purpose
in life as well.

A Universal Tenet

Every life, regardless of our
beliefs, accomplishments,
appearance, or genus, is
equal, important, and meaningful.

Most of humanity's struggles
result from not understanding
this universal tenet, believing
instead, not only are we
superior to all other forms
of life, but some lives are
more important than
others as well.

The World We See

How we view life's challenges
will decide our destiny.
If we only see darkness,
we will spend our lives
fearful, never truly
experiencing the reason
for our life's journey.

If, however, we see light,
not only in the world,
but within all others as
well, we will fully embrace
life, and, in doing so,
discover our true purpose
in life as well.

The Universe

In the vastness of space,
the universe contains
celestial bodies and wonders
too abundant to tally.

Alone, isolated from others,
though their impact may be
significant, their existence
and importance in the
universe is nominal.

Only together, as part of
a solar system, galaxy,
the cosmic web, will its
intention be fully realized.

Meaning

Meaning may not
be found in a self-
centered world.

It must first be
discovered within,
then selflessly shared,
without reason or
favor, with all others.

The Waterfall

In early spring, water melting
from faraway mountain peaks,
rush downward to the valley below.
Before it reaches its destination,
the water is calm, peaceful.
It is only when it descends
over an elevated bluff, its
intensity increases, as it
produces a beautiful,
majestic waterfall.

Humanity may be contrasted
to a waterfall.
Before we are born we are
calm, peaceful, wise, knowing
only unconditional love.
It is not until we enter the
world, socialized to accept
the self-centered beliefs of
society, our understanding
about life's purpose
becomes distorted.

The true irony of life is
we then spend the rest of
our lives, trying to return
to the calm, peaceful reflections
and feelings of love we once
knew before we were first born.

Givers and Takers

There are two types of
people: givers and takers.
A giver is someone who
shares their love freely
with all others, wanting
only the best for everyone.
A taker worries only about
themselves, unafraid to
take advantage of another.

Though a taker may be
successful in life, they
will never experience true
love, inner peace or learn
the lessons we are alive
to understand.

A giver, however, will
find these in abundance,
while also discovering life's
genuine intentions as well.

We Are Stronger Together

When you are down,
struggling to hold
on, I will be there.
It matters not if
we know each other.
I will always offer my
hand to hold you, my
love to embrace you,
and my soul to
caress your wounds.

We are stronger together.
If you ever wondered
why we are born,
this is the reason.
To selflessly help and
love each other in
our time of need.

The Ceiling

Above me the ceiling limits
my view of the world,
restricting my vision.
I realize, above its confines,
lies an extraordinary
unrestricted realm,
waiting to embrace me
with its inherent wisdom
and unconditional love.

Like the ceiling, most of
us limit our view of the
world, only believing what
we were taught, seeing our
life limited by its boundaries.
It is only when we observe
what is above the ceiling,
by challenging our self-
centered beliefs, the
beauty and genuine
possibilities life offers
may truly be discovered.

Our False Beliefs

There are many who
believe they are leading
a successful, purposeful
life, accomplishing everything
they were taught would
allow them to do so.
Though they may be
wealthy, famous, have
many material possessions,
nothing achieved in a self-
centered world, unless
shared to benefit others,
will bring genuine success
or purpose to our lives.

Success and purpose may
only be found when we
share our innate wisdom
and unconditional love,
our spirit, to help others
become successful and
discover meaning in
their lives as well.

We Are All Children of the World

Regardless of the color
of our skin, ethnicity,
religion, whether we are
rich or poor, famous or
unknown, or any other
comparison we may
make, we are all
children of the world.
No one life, regardless
of our differences or
accomplishments, is
or ever has been
better, more important,
than another's.

Apart, though some
may be more successful,
we will all fail.
Only together, by putting
our trivial differences
aside, may we all
flourish, and discover
genuine meaning in
our lives as well.

The Bird

Soaring in the sky, wings
outstretched, gracefully
riding the currents of wind,
the bird majestically
embraces is destiny.
The higher the bird climbs,
the more difficult its
journey, due to the thin
air and lack of oxygen.

When it remains close to
the ground, it feels secure
in its environment.
It is only when the bird
challenges its confines though,
soaring high above, will it
truly see the world below,
discovering the genuine
beauty of life.

Humanity is very
much like the bird.
When we remain in our
comfort zone, fearing to soar
and challenge our self-centered
beliefs, we will never see
life's true potential.
It is only when we rise

above, confront our fears,
climb to new heights, may
we begin a quest to
understand our true
life's purpose.

The Sun

As the sun rises, our
life begins anew.
With our birth, the sheer
beauty and clarity of all
it illuminates is apparent.
With our exposure to the world,
however, the suns brilliance
begins to fade, as its light
is partially hidden behind
the clouds above.

For some, only a few clouds
exist, allowing the sun's
rays to periodically reach
the ground below.
For others though, the clouds
darken, covering the entire sky.

How overcast the skies become
depends on our acceptance of
all we learned to be true.
Those who have fully
embraced this truth, though
they may find success in the
world, will perpetually live
under a darkened overcast
sky, one where the sun's
rays are seldom seen.

Only those who start to
challenge their self-centered
beliefs will begin to see
the clouds dissipate.
Though few will ever
observe the crystal clear
blue sky we once observed
with our birth, the journey
to see once again an
unblemished blue sky
is what makes life
truly worthwhile.

Listen

Listen to the quiet in
between the words
of another to hear
the genuine meaning.

It is then you will sense
their essence speaking
silently, as it converses
with our spirit within.

See Beyond

See beyond the façade
we each project, to
the essence within.

It is here the answers
about life's true purpose
lie and the genuine
worth of another
may be discovered.

Finding Meaning

Open your heart.
Change the world.
Find purpose.
Help all in need without
motive or benefit.
Selflessly share your
innate wisdom and
unconditional love
with others.

This is the meaning
of life; the reason
for our life's journey.

Our Common Purpose

Though we each pursue
our own path through life,
we all have the same
purpose: to reunite with
our spirit within, then
share its essence selflessly
with all others, so they
too may discover their
life's genuine purpose as well.

The Beauty of Life

Every life is beautiful,
perfect in every way.
Appearance or any
other comparisons
mean little.

The beauty of life resides
not on the outside.
It only lies within,
where the true beauty
and worth of another
has always been.

Tears

My sorrow is inconsolable.
Tears steadily fall down
my face as I see the pain
and torment of so many.
Hunger, prejudice, senseless
deaths, ending their life
before their appointed time.
Every meaningless death
harms all; their spirit no
longer present to spread
its innate wisdom and
unconditional love with others.

My tears surge for all,
realizing these man-made
challenges never need occur.
We are alive to help,
not harm another.
My tears will continue
to flow until humanity awakens,
mitigating the devastating
struggles and premature
death of so many innocents.

The Power of Love

The greatest power in
the universe is love,
shared selflessly with all.
It matters not if we know
another or if they are strangers.

We are alive to share our
unconditional love, present
within each, to benefit all.

The Aurora

The picturesque colorful
lights dance in the night
sky, powered by solar
wind speeding through
the earth's atmosphere.
Most are unable to see
this spectacular display,
as it is generally only
seen at the extreme
corners of our planet.

Despite where we live
though, we each may be
able to see an aurora
in our life as well.
To do so, we must light
up our darkened core,
by traveling to the
far corners within.

We may do this by
selflessly sharing the
wisdom and unconditional
love of our spirit within,
then allowing it to guide
all of our life's choices.

A Moment of Sanity

We live in a chaotic self-
obsessed world, struggling
to survive the onslaught
of daily challenges.
To endure in such a world,
we must rely on ourselves
and what we need
to do to survive.

Every once in a while,
though, a passing thought
may penetrate our protective
exterior, our façade,
questioning our beliefs
and path through life.

This brief awakening creates
a moment of unbelievable
calm, inner peace, and
feelings of authentic love,
as a glimpse of what
discovering genuine
meaning in our life
reveals itself.

After We Awaken

There may come a time
in our life we begin to
question the self-centered
beliefs we were taught and
blindly accepted as true.
Once this happens, we may
never fall back asleep by
continuing to follow
the status quo.

The matrix we once lived
in begins to dissolve as
our life changes forever.
We now see our friends,
family, job, and everything
else in the world through
different eyes.
The trivialities of life no
longer interest us, as we
discover we now have
little in common with
those who remain asleep.

It is a time of great change,
one where we begin to
understand, we are alive
not simply to find our own
success and survive in

the world, but to selflessly
help all others, despite
our differences or
accomplishments,
do so as well.

Our Search For Meaning

There are but two paths
through life we may choose.
Depending on our choice,
we each decide our destiny.

The first path is the self-
centered path of the ego,
learned after our birth.
There are numerous choices
we may pursue if we
follow its direction.
Though some lead to having
a successful life, none of
them will help us find real
meaning or purpose in our life.

To understand the genuine
reason for our life's journey,
we must follow the second path:
that of the spirit, a piece of
god present within every life.
By following our spirit's
guidance and sharing its
wisdom and unconditional
love with others, all our
questions will be answered,
and we will discover the
true meaning of life as well.

The Paradox of Life

When we live life worrying
only about ourself, though we
may be successful, able to
enjoy life to the fullest, as
death approaches and we
review our life, almost
all will begin to question
if their success meant their
life was important and meaningful.

As most begin to realize it
was not, the paradox of
life becomes evident.
Though it is too late for
them to change, they
finally understand, life
was never just about them.
Rather, their success was
meant to be selflessly shared
to help others become
successful in life as well.

Our Most Important Designation

Most believe we are the
labels we assign to each
other: male, female, wealthy,
poor, black, white, or any
number of other descriptions
we use to differentiate and
define ourselves in the world.

Though these labels are used
to describe who we are in a
self-centered world, they ignore
our most important designation.
We are spirit, a piece of god
encased in a human body,
intimately connected to each other.

The genuine purpose of our
life's journey has little to do
with our other designations.
We are alive to selflessly
share our spirit's inherent
wisdom and unconditional
love with all others, so
everyone, regardless of our
differences or challenges in
life, may discover their true
purpose in life as well.

Life's Genuine Value

We are alive to discover,
spiritually flourish, share
our inherent wisdom and
unconditional love, present
within every life, with all
others, so they too may
discover their true
purpose in life as well.

Separate, our lives lack purpose.
Only together, selflessly sharing
our spirit's wisdom and love
with others may we all succeed
and discover life's genuine value.

Our Ego's Motive

We are meant to sincerely
love, care, help, and trust
each other, not hate, neglect,
hinder, and fear others.
Allowing our lives to be
guided by our spirit, inherent
within every life, will bring
inner peace, authentic love,
and genuine meaning to our lives.

Continuing, however, to permit
the ego, our self-centered beliefs,
to control our life, will instead
lead to the unsustainable
continuation of the status quo.

We awaken when we begin
to question the ego's motives.
We become enlightened when
we genuinely understand, its
real motives are self-serving,
and little of what we
learned was true.

Our Spirit Will Endure

Though we may be successful
in life, wealthy, famous,
have many possessions, if
our accomplishments and
prosperity are not shared
with others less fortunate,
including those we do not
know, then we will have
lived our life without purpose.

Only by selflessly helping
others, without motive or
benefit, will our spirit endure
in everyone we influenced
and helped with our
kindness and generosity.
Doing so, will also bring
genuine understanding
and meaning to our
life's journey as well.

This is How an Enlightened Soul Sees the World

A deep azure sky, no clouds
to obstruct our view.
Colorful fragrant flowers
and trees blossoming
for all to enjoy.
A calm ocean, barely a
ripple disturbing its
gentle surface.
Peace, love, kindness,
replacing war, hate, injustice.

Selflessly helping everyone,
treating each with
a warm embrace.
Recognizing every life
is equally important.
Observing no differences
between us, regardless
of our distinct beliefs.
Aiding all, without
hesitation, through their
struggles, so they too may
see the world through
these eyes as well.

Only Together May We All Flourish

Every soul regardless of our
differences, accomplishments,
or genus, deserves to be
helped in their time of need,
and treated with unconditional
love, selflessly shared
without motive or benefit.
There is never a reason to do otherwise.

No one is, or ever has been
better, their life more
important, than another's.
We will never understand
our life's genuine purpose
unless we realize only together
may we all flourish.
Apart, regardless how
successful our life has been,
it will have been led
without meaning or purpose.

Our Innate Wisdom

Listen silently, in
between your thoughts.
Hear the messages within.
The wisdom of the universe
resides there, including the
purpose for our life's journey.
Everything else is an illusion.

To awaken, embrace
the wisdom and loving
messages you are offered,
then selflessly share them
to help others do so as well.

The Sky

On a clear day, we may
see far away mountains as
we gaze at the azure sky.
The purity of our view is
unobstructed; no impediments
obscure our vision.

Humanity may be
contrasted to the sky.
When we allow our acquired
self-centered beliefs and opinions
to cloud our lives, our vision
is obstructed as life's
challenges overwhelm us.
For some, their view is
so impeded, they are
nearly blind, unable
to see anything but
hate, fear, anger.

On those days though, when
we let down our shield, allowing
our spirit within to influence
our decisions, the sky once
again starts to brighten, as
we begin a quest to rediscover
the genuine path through life
we were always meant to follow.

We Are One Spirit

Though we are many, appear,
believe differently, we share
a unifying spirit, a piece of
god present within each,
inextricably connecting
us to each other.

Separate, we will fail.
Only together, selflessly
helping each other, will
we all succeed and live
a life of genuine meaning
and purpose.

Two Choices

We each have two pathways
through life we may follow.
The first is to embrace everything
we learned as we were socialized
to accept the self-centered
beliefs of the world.
This path is the cause of many
of humanity's problems, including
war, hunger, climate change;
hate, prejudice, inequity.

Pursuing the spiritual path
is the second choice we
may follow instead.
Though it is much more
challenging, it will lead to
inner peace, and to
discovering authentic love
and purpose in our life.

This path though, may not be
found in a self-centered world.
To discover its location, gaze
within, listen quietly, then
fully embrace the wisdom
and unconditional loving
messages you hear.

Only Together May We Find Meaning

A small part of god exists
within every life, inextricably
connecting each to the other.
Apart we are weak, lost,
existing, though not truly
not living or experiencing
life as it was meant to be.

If we live our life like this,
though we may have been
successful and accomplished
much in our life, our life will
end without discovering
authentic love or the
genuine reason for
our life's journey.

Only together, selflessly
helping each other will
our lives be truly worthwhile
and the true meaning
of life be understood.

Our Spirit Lives Forever

Death is not the end.

When our physical body
perishes, if we had selflessly
shared our spirit's wisdom
and unconditional love with
others while we were alive,
our spirit will remain long
after our death, as part of
the spirit of all those whose
path we crossed and life
we had positively affected.

The impact we had on others,
will then be passed by them
to those they meet as
well in perpetuity.

What is Success?

Wealth, fame, career, family,
material possessions, or
anything else we were told
will bring us success,
will not do so.
True success may not be
found in a self-centered world.

It may only be discovered by
embracing our spirit within,
then selflessly sharing its
inherent wisdom and
unconditional love to help
others become successful
in their life as well.

Our Beliefs

Everything we learn about
success, happiness, and
meaning in our life, and
accept as true after we are
born is the underlying cause
of many of humanity's
self-inflicted problems,
challenges, and harmful emotions.

We awaken when we begin
to question our self-
centered beliefs.

We become enlightened
when we genuinely understand
the truth of this tenet.

We Are One People

Regardless of any
differences, no one is,
or ever has been,
better, more important
than another.
It matters not our race,
ethnicity, religion; nor
our wealth, fame, career.

We are one people.
Only together, selflessly
helping each other, will
we all discover our
true purpose in life.

Every Life is Important

Humanity believes since
they are the dominant species
on our planet, their life is
more important than other
less evolved life forms.
There are some who even
believe, the lives of those
who are different than them,
as not as valuable as theirs.

This self-centered view of
the world is the cause of
many of humanity's self-
inflicted problems, harmful
emotions, and actions,
throughout their domination
on our planet.

In reality, every life,
regardless of genus,
appearance, or
accomplishments, is
equally important.
Only when humanity
starts to understand this,
may their spiritual
evolution truly begin.

When We See Another

When we see another, do
we look at their physical
body or the presence within each?
Our form is but a shell,
sheltering a spirit, a piece
of god within, present to
help guide our life with
its innate wisdom and
unconditional love, to
provide meaning and
purpose in our lives.

Those who only see our
physical self, believing its
appearance defines us,
though their life may be
successful and their body
pleasant to view, will lead
a life without purpose or meaning.

Only those who peer deeply
into the eyes, the soul of
another, seeing beyond
their superficial physique
and façade they present
to the world, will truly
discover another's
genuine worth.

Absolute Love

Anger, hate, prejudice,
and all harmful negative
emotions are learned.
They do not exist until
after our birth, exposure,
and acceptance of the beliefs
living in a self-centered
world encourage.

Absolute love, shared
freely, unconditionally,
with all others, is the
only genuine emotion
we are meant
to recognize.
It awaits within every
life, waiting our
permission to be
released.

With this consent we
awaken, beginning our
journey toward enlightenment.

Light or Darkness

We each decide whether we
will embrace light or darkness.
Though both will remain
with us throughout our
life's journey, it is a choice
which path we will
primarily follow.

Those who embrace darkness
accept all they learned,
suppressing their natural
inherent loving tendencies.

Those, however, who primarily
see light, will not only
understand life's genuine
purpose, but bring true
change to the world as
well by brightly shining
their light on others.

We Must Help Each Other

Every life is equally
deserving to be helped
in times of need; no one
should ever be ignored.
Hunger, poverty, prejudice,
and many of humanity's
self-inflicted struggles and
challenges in life are human
creations, resulting from
believing some are more
deserving than others;
they are not.

Only when humanity truly
realizes this, may our world
evolve, allowing us to begin
on a quest to discover our
genuine purpose in life.

Helping Others Tirelessly

Those who have awoken,
sensing the first messages
of their spirit within,
must tirelessly help
others awaken as well.

Though we may have
discovered our true
purpose in life, our lives
will be incomplete if we
do not help others do
so as well.

Why Are We Alive?

Numerous philosophers,
religious leaders, and many
others have attempted to
answer the question:
why are we alive?
The best answer I have
found is: we are alive to
reunite with our spirit
within, then share its
infinite wisdom and
unconditional love
with all others.

Any other explanation is
a deception, fostered by
the ego, our learned beliefs,
to make our life's journey
more challenging.

The Reason for Our Existence

Within each life, two different,
often quite contrary entities,
compete for dominance:
the ego, our self-centered
beliefs, and the spirit, a piece
of god present to give our
lives meaning by sharing its
wisdom and unconditional
love to help guide
our life's choices.

Those who embrace the
beliefs of the ego remain
asleep, trapped in the matrix,
an illusion of reality.
It is only when we allow
the spirit to be our primary
guide in life that life's
genuine meaning becomes
evident, and the reason
for our existence understood.

The Good in Others

Beyond the pretense we
created when we were
young, lies the purity of
our spirit present within each.
Though in many it may be
hidden by the dominance
of their self-centered
beliefs, it remains with
us until our demise.

To help bring genuine
change to the world, see
beyond the façade of others,
seeking only the good
in them instead.

What Do You See?

When you look at another,
do you see their appearance,
race, ethnicity, or any
other differences there
may be between us?
Do you hear their spoken
words or sense the genuine
meaning behind their dialogue?
Do you judge them,
justifying your superiority,
or do you accept them
as your equal?

Those who view others
through their self-centered
opinions remain asleep,
living in a matrix, created
by the ego, our learned beliefs.

Those, however, who see
beyond our differences,
understanding the true worth
of another is within, have
awoken, beginning their
quest to discover life's
true purpose.

The Reason We Are Alive

There are many who
wonder why we are alive?
Is it to become wealthy,
famous, be able to enjoy
the best things life offers?
If you believe this, though
your goals may come true,
you will have ignored the
genuine reason for
our life's journey.
Nothing found in a self-
centered world will
answer this question.

In reality, we are alive to
reunite with our spirit within,
then selflessly share its
inherent wisdom and
boundless love with
others, so they too may
remember their purpose
in life as well.

The Path to Enlightenment

There are some who have
awoken to the possibility
everything they learned as
they were growing up
may not be true.
Once this doubt begins,
they will never again be
able to believe the illusions
they once accepted as real.

As they travel along the
path toward enlightenment,
they begin to view the world
differently; their self-centered
view of life radically changes.

Instead of being only concerned
for their own survival and
success, they now are
equally worried about
the survival and success
of others as well.

A Well Lived Life

It is not how long you live
or what you acquire when
you are alive that determines
if your life is successful.

Rather, a life has been well
lived if you are able to
embrace your true destiny,
by accepting and sharing
your loving spirit's
compassion and wisdom
with all others.

How We View Life

We each have a choice
how we see others.
We may see the beauty in
them or the loathsomeness.

Those who only see the
latter, though they may have
lived a successful life, it
will have been without
experiencing true happiness,
love, or meaning.

Those, however, who see
beyond the superficial
layers, the façade, others
erect, to the spirit within
each, will have found these
things in abundance and
discovered the genuine
meaning of life as well.

See Only the Good

See the good in others;
disregard the rest.

Though we all have flaws,
adopted when we were
young, embrace instead
the spirit within each,
thereby awakening their
spirit to the genuine
possibilities life
truly offers.

The Genuine Purpose of Life

Selflessly sharing our
innate wisdom and
unconditional love,
present within each,
with all others, is the
genuine purpose of life.

Anything else, thought
to be significant and
bring meaning to our
lives, is an illusion,
fostered by our self-
centered upbring,
to challenge our
choices in life.

Our Desired Destination

The cause of many of
humanity's problems and
needless struggles in the
world, is from living in
a competitive society,
one where the importance
of the individual is greater
than the needs of all others.

Even the partial acceptance
of these self-centered beliefs,
prevent those who have
awoken, from traveling
further on their path
toward enlightenment.

It is only when we truly
realize and accept the
complete fiction of these
ideas, instead embracing
the need to unconditionally
share, help, and love all
others, that we will be
able to move closer to
our desired destination.

The Realization

With the realization
genuine happiness,
love, and meaning,
may not be found in
a self-centered world
without first discovering
it within, we awaken,
beginning an enduring
journey to understand
our true purpose in life.

The Guru

One does not need a guru,
a spiritual teacher, to
understand spirituality.
Though the sage may have
traveled further on the path
toward enlightenment,
within each person, the
identical wisdom is, and
has always existed.

Humanity's greatest spiritual
leaders, Jesus, Mohammed,
and Buddha, understood this.
We each may join these
gurus in their desire to
selflessly help others,
by embracing our own
spiritual core, present
within each, allowing
it to be the primary
guide in our life.

The Problem With the Ego

The ego represents everything
we are taught, believe, and
accept is true from the
moment of our birth.
It exists to protect us from
others who wish us harm,
and to bolster our feelings
of self-worth; it also helps
us survive in a self-centered
competitive world.

When it is successful,
we believe our life is
meaningful and rich.
In reality though,
this is not true.
For the ego also
suppresses the spirit,
present within each life.
By doing so, it prevents
us from understanding
our life's true purpose as well.

As Death Approaches

Many go through life asleep,
believing everything they
were taught is true.
Though they may become
wealthy, famous, have a
prestigious job, they will
never experience true
love or know the genuine
reason they were granted life.

As death approaches, when
they review their life, they
may finally understand their
wealth, fame, job, were not
very important and did
not define who they truly are.

It is then they may finally
understand, we are spirit,
alive to selflessly share our
spirit's innate wisdom and
unconditional love to help
all others understand who
they truly are as well.

Living Life in Fear or Love

We each choose whether
we will live in fear
or with love.
Those who live in fear,
with the countless other
harmful emotions and
problems caused by its
acceptance, though they
may have had a successful
life, be wealthy, famous,
have many possessions,
if their success was not
selflessly shared to benefit
others, their life will
have been led without
purpose or meaning.

Only those selflessly aiding
all in need, though they
may be poor, struggling
to survive if they share
their unconditional love
to benefit others, who
will discover the true
meaning of life.

Spiritual Debt

Harm to another in any
manner adds to our
spiritual debt, making
it more difficult to truly
understand the reason
for our life's journey.

Only by selflessly sharing
our innate wisdom and
unconditional love to
benefit others, may this
balance lessen, as we
begin on a journey to
understand our true
purpose in life.

Why Are We Alive?

We are alive to selflessly
help each other without
motive or benefit.
Every life, regardless
of our differences or
accomplishments in
life, is equally valuable.

Understanding this
is the reason for
our life's journey.

Treat Others With Kindness

Any slight to another,
regardless of form,
harms both.
Every interaction not
predicated on kindness,
weakens our world and
our ability to discover
life's genuine purpose.

Always treat everyone,
regardless of differences,
with unconditional love.
Doing so, will not only
help further the spiritual
evolution of our planet,
but also allow each of
us to experience true
happiness, inner peace,
and discover the genuine
meaning of life as well.

The Genuine Reason for Our Life's Journey

All life, both on our planet
and in the universe itself,
is tethered by a universal
spirit, a piece of god,
present within each.

Every life, therefore,
regardless of our
differences, genus,
or accomplishments,
is equally important,
each having a piece
of god within.

Selflessly sharing our
spirit's wisdom and
unconditional love for
the benefit of all others
is the genuine reason
for our life's journey.

Humanity's Indifference

Living life, worried only
about ourselves is not
only the cause of much
of our worry and internal
stress, but also many of
humanity's problems and
hardships as well.

These challenges result
from accepting our beliefs,
convincing us meaning
in our life may be found
in a self-centered world;
it may not.

We may only begin to
mitigate the stress and
challenges caused by
humanity's indifference,
by sincerely helping and
caring about each other
so all may benefit, thrive,
and discover meaning in
their lives as well.

Undoing the Damage

When we are first born,
the damage begins.
As we learn what is
expected of us, we
start to accept the
self-centered beliefs
of the world around us.
For most, these beliefs
impede the underlying
messages of their spirit,
a piece of god, present
within each of us.

Though the ego will
always remain, helping
us survive in the world,
only by allowing the spirit,
rather than the ego, to be
the primary guide in our
life, will the damage
which began were young,
be mitigated, and the
genuine purpose of our
life's journey be understood.

Taking Advantage of Others

There is never a reason
to do, say, or imply
harm to another.
It matters not if the
slight is verbal, physical,
or in any other manner.
We are all in life's
journey together.

Though many believe the
injury they caused to the
other is trivial, in reality,
it harms both.
Apart, regardless of our
success or accomplishments
in life, our lives
are insignificant.

Only together, by always
helping others and treating
all with respect and
unconditional love, will
life's genuine meaning
become apparent.

Living in a Split Reality

We live in a world where
two truths exist simultaneously.
One we can see, as we view
the constant struggles and
hardships of so many
around the world.

Those existing in this self-
centered reality, believe their
indoctrination into society,
accepting the loneliness and
numerous challenges
accompanying these
beliefs result in.

The other truth resides
within each of us, recognizing
unconditional love as its mantra.
This reality realizes only by
selflessly helping each other
will we all survive and
find purpose in our life.

Most exist living on a
continuum between these
two realities.
Only those though, who
embrace the latter, will

discover true happiness,
boundless love, inner peace,
and understand the genuine
meaning of life as well.

The Healers

There are those who try
to help others who are
struggling be able to survive
in a self-centered world.
Though this is important,
without also awakening their
spirit, their reason for being,
their help is imperfect.

To truly heal another, do
not forget the unseen
essence present within,
not only allowing someone
to survive in the world,
but also discover purpose
in their lives as well.

Why Are We Alive?

Are we alive just to survive
in the world by making money,
having material possessions,
enjoying the things we were
told would bring joy and
meaning to our lives?
Or is there another reason?

Though some have
achieved their goals,
their life was only
partially lived.
Without also recognizing and
sharing their spirit's innate
wisdom and unconditional
love, present within every
life, though successful, their
life was led without ever
discovering their true
purpose in life.

Our Primary Decision Maker

Within every life lies a
spirit, a piece of god
inextricably connecting
each life to the other's.
For most their spirit soon
assumes an inferior position,
forgotten, silenced by
their dominating self-
centered beliefs.

We awaken when
we first begin to
sense our spirit within.
As we slowly allow the
spirit to become our
primary decision maker,
our journey to
enlightenment may
truly begin.

Needless Death

Every senseless death
must be mourned.
Whether the loss was
due to violence, starvation,
hardship, or any other
preventable means, each
life is precious; their early
demise robbing the world
of their loving spirit.

It matters not if we know
the person who perished.
We are all intimately
connected, each having
a spirit, a piece of god within.
The premature death of any
life, will therefore be
universally suffered by all.

Life's Genuine Intentions

When we are asleep, we
believe and accept all
we learned is true.
Though we may be
successful, if that success
is not selflessly shared with
others, we are living an
illusionary life, unaware
of the matrix we exist in.

We begin to awaken when
we question if there is more
to life than what we see
and were taught.
We become enlightened
when we understand nothing
in the matrix is real; the only
reality lies within each of us.

Selflessly sharing our spirit's
inherent wisdom and
unconditional love will
not only shatter the matrix,
but reveal life's genuine
intentions as well.

Our Focus in Life

Besides the basic challenges
of survival: shelter, safety,
and sustenance, we each
may be exposed to many
other difficult situations
in our life as well.

Our upbringing emphasizes
achievement to define our
purpose; money, material
possessions, our importance
in the world defines that success.
This emphasis is not only the
cause of many of humanity's
self-inflicted struggles, but
also of many challenges
in our life as well.

After our basic needs are
met, our focus in life must
shift to selflessly helping
all others meet their
basic needs as well.
This is the path humanity
was always meant to
pursue; the lesson
we are alive to learn.

The World of Enlightenment

Imagine a world where
people, all other forms of
life, and our planet were
more important than money.
Where instead of competition,
there was cooperation.
Greed would be replaced
by generosity, war replaced
by peace, and hate
replaced by love.

Though you may believe
this is a fantasy, it is
quite the opposite.
In truth, it is living in a
self-centered world
that is the true fiction.

Humanity's original purpose,
disguised by our learned
beliefs, is to fully embrace
our spiritual center within,
then selflessly share our
spirit's innate wisdom and
unconditional love to help
all others rediscover
their spiritual center as well.

The Journey Back

Every life is accompanied
by a spirit, a piece of god
present within each.
Following our spirit's guidance
and sharing its inherent
wisdom and unconditional
love with others, will allow
us to live a life of genuine
meaning and purpose.

It is not until after we are
born and exposed to the
views of the world, we
adopt the self-centered beliefs
we are taught, enabling us to
survive the many challenges
in life we may face.
Though some of what we
learn is necessary, most is
a distraction, mitigating our
ability to discover the genuine
reason we were born.

We are born enlightened.
We then are socialized to
accept society's norms.
Then we often spend the
rest of our life trying to

desperately return to the
peaceful, loving state we
once knew before we
were first born.

What is Normal?

It is not normal to live
in a world of greed,
prejudice, inequity; of
hunger, war, homelessness.
Accepting living in such
a world is considered
normal by many;
it is not.

The normal world we are
supposed to live in is a
world of love, compassion,
and equality, one where
we help each other
in times of need.

Only when humanity
redefines its definition
of normal and truly
understands this, may
the spiritual evolution
of our planet finally begin.

We're So Vain

Humanity believes their
lives are more important
than all other forms of
life, and the planet that
enables their survival.
They even believe, the
lives of some, due to their
race, ethnicity, wealth, or
any number of other
differences, are more
valuable than others.

This arrogant view of the
world is the cause of many
of humanity's problems.
War, hunger, prejudice,
inequity, are just a few of
the numerous challenges
resulting from the belief
in their superiority.

After we awaken, sensing
the first messages from our
spirit within, we begin to
question these beliefs.
With the realization every
life, each with a spirit, a
piece of god within, is equally

important and must be respected and helped in their time of need, we begin in earnest our journey to discover the genuine meaning of life.

Spiritual Love

Spiritual love, inherent
within each life, is shared
without expectation to
comfort another in
their time of need.

Freely sharing this
universal loving bond
with others is the lesson
we are alive to learn.

The Message

Some spend their lives
hoping to hear a message
telling them what their
purpose in life is.
It is very difficult, though,
to hear this message as it
is often hidden behind layers
of beliefs we learned and
accepted as true when
we were young.

There may come a time in
our life though, we begin to
sense a quiet message within,
trying to be heard.
When the message finally
becomes clear, we realize
almost everything we were
taught was an illusion, meant
to distract us from our
true purpose in life.

With this realization, inner
peace, genuine happiness, and
true love, will encompass our
entire being, as the genuine
purpose of our life's
journey is understood.

See Beyond Our Differences

Though we are all
different in many
ways, it is our similarities
that must unite us.
Look beyond appearance,
beliefs, accomplishments,
to see the genuine soul,
the essence of another.

If you do, you will find
we are truly one, united
by a universal spirit,
intimately connecting
us to each other.
Despite our many
differences, we each
have a small piece
of god within.
Recognizing this common
bond, unites us all
together as one.

Love Unites Us

Though we all look and
believe differently, it is love
that unites us as one.
Intimately linked together
by a unifying spirit present
within each, our life's quest
is to selflessly share our
unconditional love with
all others, helping each
in their time of need.

To discover life's genuine
purpose, open your heart,
and release your infinite love
within, for the benefit all.

Together

I am but a fellow traveler
on the journey through life.
Though I may appear and
view life differently than
you, we must put aside
our differences to
help each other.

Only together may we
both succeed and discover
the genuine reason for
our life's journey.

I Am God

I am god, your spirit.
A small part of me lives
within everything alive.
Since I exist within all
forms of life, no one
person or life form is,
or ever has been better,
more important than another's.

Every life is intended
to selflessly share my
presence, wisdom, and
unconditional love,
with all others.
Apart, worrying just
about yourself, your
life will lack purpose.

Only together, helping
each other, respecting
every life and the planet
I bequeathed you, will
you discover me and
understand the genuine
reason you were granted life.

Judging Others

In the self-centered world
we live in, many judge and
demean others due to their
race, ethnicity, beliefs,
or any number of
other differences we
use to justify our
superiority to another.
They, therefore, often
ignore and treat those
they feel inferior with
indifference.

When we awaken,
sensing the first messages
from our spirit within,
we realize no one life,
regardless of
accomplishments,
appearance, or any
other possible comparison,
each with a spirit, a piece
of god within, is or every
has been, more important
than another's.

Our Spirit Will Live On

When we die, only our
body and ego perishes.
Our spirit, however, which
accompanies each life,
lives on forever.
Its essence returns to a
higher frequency, one
where only peace and
unconditional love
are present.

Our spirit, though, also
continues to live on in
all those we positively
influenced during our
life, when we selflessly
shared its innate wisdom
and love to help others
in their time of need.

Our spirit will therefore
remain part of them
until their death.
And then, it will also
remain a part of all those
they positively influenced
during their life as well.

The Matrix We Created

We are alive to
selflessly help
each other through
life's many challenges,
by sharing our excess
and unconditional love
to ease others' burdens.

Anything else is simply
an illusion, fostered by
the matrix we created,
after we were born.

Why is There?

Why is there hate,
prejudice, hunger, and
numerous other struggles
experienced by so many?
Why is there a sense of
entitlement, feeling some
are superior, their life
more important than
another's, due to
their differences or
accomplishments
in life?

Though we look, act,
believe differently, we
are all one, intimately
linked by a universal
spirit, a piece of god
present within each.
No one life is or ever
has been better
than another's.

Only when humanity
truly understands this,
may the needless struggles
be mitigated, and our
planet's spiritual evolution
finally begin.

Helping Each Other

We are alive to help,
not harm each other.
Yet, due to our self-
centered upbringing,
we have forgotten
the reason for our
life's journey.

We awaken when
we begin to hear
the first messages
from our spirit within
reminding us of our
true purpose in life.

We become enlightened
when we fully embrace
its inherent wisdom and
unconditional loving
beliefs, then selflessly
share those to help
all in need.

Look Past the Pain

Every life should
always be treated
with reverence, even
if the other person
caused you grievance.

Look past the insult
and the pain to the
authentic person,
present within each.

Forgive the injury,
realizing the cause
of their indiscretion
is their protective self,
not the genuine soul
before you.

A World of Kindness, Empathy, and Love

How can we accept the
senseless demise of another;
the hunger, lack of shelter,
or any other needless struggles
suffered by anyone?
All these hardships
need not exist.
They are caused by living
in a self-centered world of
greed, prejudice, and entitlement.

Our planet is careening
toward an abyss, one we
may not be able to prevent
our descent into.
We may only reverse
this inevitable outcome,
by sincerely helping and
loving each other,
assuring every person,
regardless of our
differences, may survive,
and be able to thrive in
a world of kindness,
empathy, and love.

Finding Love and Happiness

We search the world to
find love and happiness.
Though we may believe
we have found them,
often they are temporary,
fleeting, like a passing
storms rain.

These things may not
be found in a self-
centered world.
To find genuine love
and happiness, look within,
then selflessly share your
love and happiness to
help others find them
in their life as well.

Every Life is Equally Valuable

There are some who
believe, due to their
race, religion, wealth,
job, or any of hundreds
of other differences,
their life is more
important than another's.
This is true not only of
humanity, but also their
beliefs about all other
forms of life as well.

Peer deeply into
the eyes of another
sentient life form.
If you do, you will see
their spirit, the same
piece of god present
within us, intimately
linking us all together.

Every life, therefore,
regardless of their
accomplishments,
appearance, or
form, each with a
piece of god within,
is, and has always
been, equally valuable.

The Truth

The truth is nothing
we learn, or is found
in the self-centered world,
even things considered
good or positive, will
bring us true happiness
or the answers we seek.

Genuine truth may only
be found within, then
must be selflessly shared
to help others find
the truth as well.

You Are Beautiful

It matters not your
appearance, the color
of your skin, your
acceptance by society,
or any other possible
comparison we may
choose to differentiate
us from another.

You are beautiful just
the way you are.
For within each, a spirit
lies, stunning in its pure
untainted loving beliefs,
seeing only the best and
beauty within all others.

I Love You

Words are not necessary
to show another your love.

Simply hold their hand,
listen to their thoughts,
warmly hug them when
they need support, look
deeply into their eyes,
beyond their façade, to
their soul within, to truly
let another know of
your love for them.

Open Your Eyes

How long may we close
our eyes, pretending
we do not see?
How many more years
may we continue to
ignore the pain, tears,
senseless deaths, and
struggles of others,
while we do nothing?

We must all open our
eyes, pretend no more,
selflessly helping all
in need, allowing each
to live their life with
dignity, hope, and
eternal love.

Living Without Fear

Though we may be
anxious, especially
about our safety and
obtaining the basic
necessities to survive,
we do not have to
live our life in fear.
Living in a self-centered
world, those who are
constantly afraid are
fearful of dying and
confronting life's
many challenges.

Those, however, who
release their fear,
accepting the loving
spiritual path through
life, though they too
may face the same trials,
fully embrace life every
day, and need fear
death only once.

I Am Your Spirit

I peer at the world
through your eyes
as your mind races
uncontrollably, trying
to make sense of the
world around you.
Though I desperately
try to be heard, my
messages are silenced,
drowned out by the chaotic
thoughts and worries in your life.

There may come a time
though, when you begin
to sense my presence.
If you do, your life will
never be the same again,
as you start to question
everything you once
believed to be true.

I am present within
every life; it matters
not your accomplishments,
appearance or genus.
The genuine purpose of life
is to merge your self-centered
beliefs with me, allowing

us together, to selflessly
help and share our inherent
wisdom and unconditional
love to benefit all others.

Our Untapped Potential

Every life has the same
potential as the great
religious leaders.
Buddha, Mohammed,
Jesus, and others were
men who fully embraced
their spiritual potential within.

Completely accepting this
path, the infinite possibilities
of miraculous occurrences,
the genuine abilities within
each of us, become reality.

We each may change the
world by following the path
of these extraordinary teachers,
by selflessly sharing our
spirit's inherent wisdom
and unconditional love,
as they did, to help others
discover their true
potential as well.

Our Value

Many define their value
by their accomplishments
in the world.
Money, material possessions,
their job, are but three
of many ways they consider
to determine their worth.

In reality, absolutely none
of these self-centered beliefs,
or anything else we learned,
will decide our true value.

To discover the genuine
value of a life, we must
first look within, embrace
our spiritual presence,
then selflessly share it,
without reservation,
with all others.

Our Children are Watching

Our children see, hear,
and adopt the beliefs of
the self-centered world
they are to live in.
They, therefore, learn about
hate, prejudice, greed, and
the value of worrying only
about themselves, while
ignoring the many
struggles of others.

Most of humanity's problems,
conflicts, and harmful emotions,
are the result of living
in such a world.
It need not be this way;
there is another path
we may follow:
the spiritual path.

It is one of unconditional
love, selflessly helping each
other, aiding all in
their time of need.
This path rejects the
learned egoistic views
of the world, believing
instead we are alive to

sincerely care about
each other.

Our children are watching.
Let us raise them to accept
the latter path through life,
allowing humanity to
evolve and our children
to flourish in a world
of hope, peace, and
unconditional love.

I Was Blind, But Now I See

Living in a self-centered
world, most believe what
they learn as they are
socialized to accept the
mores of society.
This narrow vision of life
blinds them to the genuine
possibilities life offers,
and is the cause of many
of humanity's self-inflicted
challenges, harmful emotions,
and needless struggles.

Only by removing our blinders,
questioning our learned beliefs,
will we begin to finally see
and understand our true
purpose in life: to selflessly
share, love, and help each
other, regardless of our
differences, through
life's many challenges.

Blaming Others

Many spend their entire
life blaming other people
and life situations for their
struggles and unhappiness,
never accepting responsibility
for their own failings.

We are all exposed to many
challenges in our lives.
It is how we respond
to them that will
determine our burden.
Those who have accepted
society's self-centered beliefs,
seldom accept blame for
their actions or struggles.

Only those who never fault
another, understanding
their experiences in life
are part of the journey,
will begin on a quest to
discover the genuine
meaning of life.

Labels

Humanity uses labels to
differentiate everyone.
Male, female, rich, poor,
black, white, Christian,
Muslim, are but a few
of the numerous ways
we distinguish ourselves
from each other.

Though some labels are
necessary to prevent
confusion, they also divide,
rather than unite us.
Prejudice, hate, feelings of
superiority, are but three of
many emotions resulting
from our inconsequential
differences.

In reality, there is but
one label that may be
used to truly describe
humanity and all life.
We are spirit, a piece of
god present within every
life, alive to selflessly share
our inherent wisdom and
unconditional love with

all others, regardless
of our differences or
accomplishments in life.

Anything else is an illusion,
created by the ego, our
learned beliefs, to challenge
our choices in life.

Living in a World of Love

View the world with love.
See only the best in others;
ignore the façade they
have created to help them
survive in a self-centered world.

If we do this, there will no
longer be greed, prejudice,
inequity; no harmful
emotions or unnecessary
struggles resulting from
living in an egoistic world.
All excess will be shared,
all judgments suspended,
all conflicts ended.

All that will be left is
unconditional love,
shared selflessly with
others, for the benefit of all.

How Many More?

How many more innocents
must die before we finally
recognize their loss?
How many more children
must needlessly perish from
war, starvation, random violence?
How much longer will we
tolerate prejudice, hate,
inequity, the endless suffering
of others, before we finally see
and do something to help
those who are struggling?

We each must answer these
questions ourselves: to
continue to accept the self-
centered status quo, or to
sincerely recognize these
harmful beliefs and actions
resulting in the challenges
of so many.

Only when we acknowledge
the truth of what is happening,
and actively attempt to correct
these injustices, may lasting
change help end these
travesties and our world
truly begin its spiritual evolution.

Freedom

We each have the freedom
to make choices in our life.
We may choose to embrace
our individual needs and
desires, even if these may
cause pain or struggle to others.

Or we may decide to help
those in need, selflessly
sharing our excess and love,
mitigating the many challenges
humanity has inflicted on itself.
We know the results of
pursuing the former path.

Perhaps it is time to sincerely
consider others in all our
words, actions, and deeds,
ensuring a future for all,
rather than continue to
be concerned only for
our own freedom.

The Reason for Life

Humanity was granted life
to accept each as equal, not
to be prejudiced of others
because of their differences;
to help, not take advantage
of others, to love, not
hate each other.

They were each given a
spirit, a piece of god, as
were all other forms of life,
to accompany them through
their life's journey, to
give their life purpose.

Instead, humanity chose to
accept their self-centered
beliefs, concerned only
for themselves, rather
than for any others.
Simply look at the world
today to see the results
of their choice.

Only when humanity accepts
the preeminence of the spirit,
rather than the ego, our learned
beliefs, will they finally understand
the true meaning of life.

Caring About Each Other

Every action we take
must not harm another.
Every word we say must
be spoken with love, not malice.
Every person we meet must
be treated with respect and
kindness, not contempt
and animosity.

There is never a reason
to do otherwise.
We are each meant to
sincerely care and help
each other through life's
many trials, not to hate
and hinder another to
benefit only ourselves.

Life's Genuine Purpose

How many people must
needlessly die before
we say no more?
How many others must
suffer, while we ignore
their pleas for help?
How many innocent children,
too young to understand why,
must go hungry, be homeless,
before we open our eyes and see?

Is one life more important
than another's?
If you believe it is, then
though you may be successful
and live to an old age, your
life will have been lived
without meaning or purpose.

If, however, you realize
every life, regardless of our
differences or accomplishments,
is equally valuable, and
selflessly share your inherent
wisdom and unconditional
love, your spirit, with each,
then you will have discovered
life's genuine purpose.

What is Our Value?

Many determine the value
of another by their wealth,
fame, job; the color of their
skin, ethnicity, religion.
Those who believe the
worth of another may be
judged by these superficial
traits, though they may be
successful, have completely
misunderstood the true
meaning of life.

There may time a time in
our life though when we
begin to question if what
we were taught and thought
to be true, really was the truth.
Only when we genuinely
understand little of it was,
may we begin to know
the true worth of another
may not be found in a
self-centered world.
Rather it may only be
discovered within each of
us, then is must be selflessly
shared to help others
understand this as well.

Is One Life More Important Than Another?

Some believe the lives of
those who are wealthy,
intelligent, have a prestigious
job, or are a certain race,
ethnicity, religion, are more
important than those who
are poor, unknown, a minority,
or working a menial job.

Absolutely none, not one of
these differences, or any
other comparisons we may
make, makes one life more
important than another's.

Every single life, regardless
of success, appearance, or
beliefs, is and has always
been, equally valuable,
each deserving to be helped
when in need, and treated
as we ourselves wish
others to treat us.

Be a Good Person

Though the world we live
in does not concern itself
with pleasantries,
emphasizing only the
needs of ourselves, rather
than others, there is never
a reason not to be kind,
considerate, to another.

Words and deeds may
severely harm someone.
Everything we say and action
we take should therefore be
shared with love, always
emphasizing the good,
rather than only
seeking out the bad.

A World of Hope

To change the world, we
each must selflessly share
our spirit, a piece of god
present within every life,
to spread its innate wisdom
and unconditional love
with all others.

It matters not our differences,
appearance, accomplishments,
or any other possible comparison
we may choose to make.
It also should not consider if
the other is someone we know
or a stranger we have never met.

Our spirit gives our lives purpose.
It accompanies each of us
through our life's journey,
inextricably linking us
to each other.

Only by sincerely helping,
caring, and loving each other,
will humanity evolve, allowing
our children to grow up in a
world of hope, rather than
continue to live in a
world of despair.

A Sensitive Heart

Living in a harsh, often
cruel self-centered world,
it is difficult to genuinely
care about another, fearful of
them one day causing us harm.
It matters not if the injury is
verbal, physical, emotional,
or any other form of suffering.

By trusting someone, we
expose our vulnerabilities,
our heart, to another.
We therefore protect ourselves
by hardening our heart, not
allowing anyone to hurt us.
Though this prevents us
from experiencing severe
pain and disappointment,
it also inhibits our genuine
feelings and emotions, hidden
within, from being shared.

To truly experience love
though, we must risk pain,
opening our vulnerable heart
to another, to allow our pure
genuine affections and
unconditional love
to be revealed.

Tribalism

Tribalism is used to justify
ones superiority over another.
These differences are the
cause of many of mankind's
self-inflicted problems and
harmful emotions.

Humanity separates itself
into tribes, castes, dividing
them in countless ways.
Race, religion, wealth, are but
three of the innumerable divides
we use to judge others.
Those who believe all they
learn about success and how
to survive in a self-centered
world, will whole-heartedly
embrace our differences.

We awaken when we begin
to question these beliefs.
We become enlightened when
we genuinely understand and
realize there are no divisions,
only commonalities.
We are all spirit, one tribe,
inextricably connected by
a universal bond, uniting
us all together as one.

The Entitled

There are some who think,
due their race, wealth, fame,
or any number of other
differences, they are better,
their life more important,
than another's.

Those who believe this,
the entitled, though they
may find success in their
life, unless they selflessly
share their success with
others, their life will have
been lived without meaning.

In truth, regardless of
our many differences
or accomplishments in
life, there are no entitled.
Every life is, and has
always been, equally important.

Sharing Your Authentic-Self

As I look at the world,
my heart is saddened by
humanity's many harmful
actions toward others.
Not one of these self-inflicted
challenges need exist.

We are alive to help each
other through life's countless
trials, by selflessly sharing
our intrinsic wisdom and
unconditional love, our
spirit, with all others.
Anything else, though we
may believe is true, is simply
an illusion, learned when
we were young, designed
to test our resolve.

To discover life's genuine
purpose, open your heart,
follow your spirit's loving
guidance, then share
your authentic-self,
to benefit all others.

What is Enlightenment?

Enlightenment is completely
accepting the spirit, the
piece of god present within
every life, as our primary
guide through life.
Our spirit's desire is to
selflessly share its inherent
wisdom and unconditional
love to help others rediscover
their spirit's yearning to
do so as well.

Though our learned self-
centered beliefs, our ego,
will always remain, they
will no longer direct our
future decisions or actions.
Only by fully accepting our
spirit's messages, will
enlightenment become reality.

If we even partially believe
otherwise, though we may
have awoken, enlightenment
will continue elude us.

One Belief

There are as many
beliefs in the world
as there are people.
Rather than unite us,
these beliefs often
divide us instead.
They are also the
underlying cause of
war, prejudice, inequity,
and innumerable other
man-made struggles.

In reality, there is but
one inherent belief that
truly defines humanity
and all life.
It is unconditional love,
shared without conditions,
to benefit all.

Let It Go

Being angry, upset at
another, harms both,
separating us from each other.
By holding onto the injury,
it inhibits our divine growth.
The insult, and our reaction
to it, results from our self-
centered vulnerabilities
we both learned when we
were young to protect us
from harmful words or
actions by another.

To be able to awaken,
and begin our spiritual
journey, we must let go
of these negative feelings,
whole-heartedly forgiving
the other for their human
failings, and embrace them,
as we do all others, with
unconditional love.

Two Realities

We live in a world where
there are two separate
distinct realities.
The first reality, accepted
by most, is the one we learn
about as we are brought up
to accept the self-centered
beliefs of the world.
Those who embrace this
reality, though they may
be successful, live to an
old age, will never truly
understand life's purpose.

The second reality, which
many are beginning to recognize,
begins when we start to
question everything we
were taught; a feeling,
we can no longer ignore,
rises from our very core.
This sensation comes from
our spirit, a piece of god
present within every life,
there to help us discover
the genuine meaning of life.

Once this happens, our life

will change forever, as we
may never return to the
former reality we once
believed to be true.

Our Human Self (Ego)

After we are born, we are
taught what to believe and
how to survive in a
self-centered world.
Though some of what we
learn is necessary to help
us survive and get along
with others, the rest are
the underlying cause of
many of humanity's
challenges in life.

When our self-centered beliefs,
our ego, dominate our life,
they often silence the quiet
messages of our spirit within.

Only when we truly embrace
our spiritual-self, relegating
our human-self to a supportive
role, as it was always meant
to be, may humanity's many
struggles be mitigated and
the spiritual evolution of
our species genuinely begin.

The Glass

The water in the crystal
clear glass is half gone.
Most see the glass partially
empty, believing before
the water nears the bottom,
they must do all the things
they were told would allow
them to be successful
and enjoy their life.
They work hard, get an
education, make money,
buy material possessions,
allowing them to be happy
before their glass empties.

The rest see the glass half
full, realizing there is much
more to learn then just
what we were taught.
They strive to refill their
glass of water to the top
by helping others realize
that most of the self-
centered views we were
brought up to believe are
true, never have been.

As their glass of water

approaches the top once
more, they understand the
genuine purpose of life is
to unconditionally love
each other, selflessly aiding
all, regardless of our differences,
so we each may fill our glass
to the top and experience a
life blessed with love, peace,
happiness, and meaning.

Our Angry Planet

Stop.
Listen.
Our world is in pain.
The earth, once pure and
untouched, now cries in
agony as it is being destroyed
by humanity's avarice.
Its rage is reflected by
worsening disasters, as the
human race thoughtlessly
pollutes its land, water, and air.

If change is not imminent,
our planet will simply wait
until our species, like so
many others, becomes extinct,
then, over time, without
humanity's uncaring presence,
it will restore its grandeur,
returning, once again, to the
pristine world it once was.

Ocoee

In the small town of Ocoee,
in the year nineteen twenty,
a carnage was unleashed
senselessly killing many
who resided there.
A group of angry people,
with light skin tone, burned
most of the town, mindlessly
killing innocents whose
only affront was their
skin color was darker.

There must never be another Ocoee.
Every single life, regardless
of our differences or beliefs,
is as important as another's.
Though we may appear,
believe, or act differently,
we are one people, intimately
connected by a spirit present
within each, alive to help
each other in our time of
need, by selflessly sharing
our love unconditionally
with others, to benefit all.

The Lighthouse

The lighthouse overlooks
the beautiful blue ocean,
its waves roaring over jagged
rocks near the sandy shore.
In the distance, the sound of
isolated vessels blare their
horns, imploring the
lighthouse to shine its bright
light toward them, so they may
avoid hitting the nearby barriers.

As with the lighthouse, we each
have a light within us as well,
present to help us avoid the
many difficult choices that
may cause us harm every day.

To discover this light, stop,
listen silently to the quiet voice
in between your chaotic thoughts,
then follow the wisdom and
unconditional loving advice
it so desperately tries
to get you to listen to.

Our Soul

A soul, accompanying every
life, is present to give
meaning to our lives.
Its craves silence from the
ego, our self-centered beliefs,
as it attempts to share its
wisdom and unconditional
love with others.

Many of humanity's self-
inflicted problems result
from its failure to hear
this message.
Though our ego will
always remain with us,
it is only when we permit
our soul to be the primary
guide in our life, will we
be able to discover the
genuine reason for
our life's journey.

Our Divisions

Humanity endlessly divides
everyone into castes,
artificially isolating us
from each other.
Race, religion, wealth,
ethnicity, are but four
of the innumerable ways
we differentiate ourselves
from others.

For those who are poor,
a minority, living in a
distant land, their destiny
is often predetermined from
the moment of their birth.
These differences serve
only to isolate us from each
other, rather than unite us.

In truth, though we may
appear, act, or believe
differently than another,
within, we are all the same.
We are spirit, alive to
understand, accept, and
embrace our spiritual core,
then selflessly share its
innate wisdom and

unconditional loving
messages to help all in need.

The Victim

We are only victims if
we allow ourselves to be.
Though others may, at times,
take advantage of us, it is
how we react that will
determine the slight.

Everyone, without exception,
has flaws, resulting from
accepting the self-centered
beliefs we were taught
when we were young.
The harm another causes us,
resulting from their upbringing,
does not represent who
they truly are.

See beyond the abuse and
the illusional façade, to the
genuine soul within another,
to realize they would never
judge or harm another.
Doing so, will permit us to
discard the pain, never allowing
us to be a victim again.

The Complainer

There are some who complain
about everything, never
learning from the lessons
they are presented.
Instead, they blame others,
bad luck, the world itself,
for their misfortunes,
struggles, and unhappiness.

Those who spend their lives
like this, though they may
find a little satisfaction if
their complaint is successful,
will never understand the
reason they were presented
these challenges, nor learn
from these opportunities.

It is only those who never
complain, embracing every
challenge life presents with
vigor, who will face the
affront and learn from
the lesson being offered.

Judging Others

Many judge others determining
their worth by their distinctions.
Judgment only divides us,
resulting in many of humanity's
challenges and harmful emotions.

Though we are all different
in many ways, we have
no right to judge another.
Each, though unique, has
a spirit, a piece of god
accompanying them
through their life's journey.

No one person, therefore,
each with a piece of god
within, is, or ever has been
better, their life more
important than another's.
Only when humanity stops
judging others, may the
spiritual evolution of our
planet finally begin.

Poison

Believing everything we
are taught about what is
expected of us, though some
may be necessary for our
survival in the world, it
is also the cause of venom
flowing through our body,
waiting an opportunity
to release its toxin.

The outcome often results
in hate, intolerance, and
violent actions.
It is also the cause of
prejudice, leading to war,
inequity, and many of
humanity's challenges.

Though our self-centered
beliefs will remain with us
throughout our life, they do
not have to dominate our actions.
By allowing our spirit, present
within each life, to be the
primary guide in our life instead,
we will embrace love rather
than hate, tolerance rather
than prejudice, and treat all

others, regardless of our differences, with respect and compassion, rather than disdain and contempt.

Who Are We?

Many believe who they are
is determined by their
circumstances in life.
Race, ethnicity, wealth, are
but a few of the hundreds of
ways we identify ourselves
in a divided world, separating,
rather than uniting us
with each other.

In truth, though we may appear,
act, and believe differently,
we are spirit, each having a
piece of god within, intimately
linking us to each other.

Our life's purpose is to put
aside our petty differences,
embrace our similarities by
accepting the wisdom and
unconditional loving guidance
of our spirit, then selflessly
sharing its messages of peace,
love, and light, with all
others, so they too may
understand and share these
messages as well.

We Are All Family

Though we may not know
someone, look or believe
differently than they do,
we are all related, connected
by a common bond,
inextricably linking
us together.

We are each part of the
extended family of humanity,
alive to help each other,
regardless of our differences,
by selflessly sharing our
inherent wisdom and
unconditional love, our
spirit, for the benefit of all.

The Right to Exist

Since humanity has dominion
over all living things on our
planet, they feel entitled to
take advantage of their weaknesses.
They therefore exploit, abuse,
and senselessly kill other life
forms, unconcerned about
their right to exist.

There are even some who
think, because of their
outward differences and
beliefs, they are more
entitled than others of
their own species as well.

Every life has a spirit, a
piece of god accompanying
it, there to give its life
purpose and meaning,
connecting each life
to the other.
It matters not its genus,
appearance, or vulnerability.

Only when humanity truly
understands this, respecting
every life's right to exist, will
its spiritual evolution truly begin.

Our Genuine Power

As we learn about the
self-centered world we
are born into, we are
taught what power is.
We are told those who
are wealthy, famous,
have an important job
that has influence over
others, are powerful.
We accept these truths,
striving to become one
of the powerful ourselves.

True power though, may
never be found in a self-
centered world; it may
only be found within.
Though some believe they
are powerful because of
their achievements, if their
power and success were not
selflessly shared to benefit
others, it was an illusion,
fostered by the ego, our
learned beliefs, to make
us believe it was real.

Intolerance

Intolerance is learned;
it is not inherent.
By judging another, we
become prejudiced, needing
to show our superiority to
others due to our differences.
Appearance, beliefs, wealth, are
but three of the numerous ways
we assess each other, needing
to prove our preeminence.

In truth, absolutely no one,
regardless of our differences
or accomplishments in life,
is better, their life more
important, than another's.
Believing we are is the
cause of many of humanity's
problems and harmful beliefs.

We are one, united by a
universal spirit, equal
in every way.
Anything else, first thought
to be true when we were young
as we were indoctrinated
into the world, is an illusion,
meant to challenge
our choices in life.

Honor Everyone

Living in a self-centered
world, concerned only for
what is best for ourself,
we tend to share ourselves
with another only if
it benefits us.
Though we may become
successful in such a world,
if our success was not
selflessly shared with
others, we will never
experience true happiness,
love, or discover
meaning in our life.

Only by truly respecting,
sharing, and honoring all
others, without focus on
ourself, will these precious
emotions be realized, allowing
us to discover our life's
genuine purpose as well.

Spiritual Philosophy

A spirit, a piece of god
accompanies each life,
intimately connecting
us to each other.
It exists to guide our lives
with its innate wisdom and
unconditional love, providing
direction and meaning in our life.

Its messages though, are often
silenced by the dominance of
the ego, our learned beliefs.
The ego's directive is self-
serving, always taking care
of itself, rather than being
concerned for others.

Meaning in life may only
arise from the spirit, whose
wisdom and loving messages
resonate when we follow its path.
Those who choose not to follow
this path, though they may
become successful, will
lead a life lacking purpose.

Only those who truly embrace
the spiritual path, relegating

the ego to a supportive role,
will discover the genuine
reason for our life's journey.

The Eclipse

The blinding sun's rays,
emerging from its luminous
core, spread throughout the
solar system, providing light,
warmth, and nourishment,
to every life in its reach.
When the moon passes directly
in front of it, blocking its light,
we wait in darkness for its return.

As with the sun, we each
have a bright light within.
When its light is unencumbered,
we feel peaceful, happy, content.
However, when our light begins
to be inhibited, eclipsed by darkness
arising from stress, struggle, or
other challenges, our dimmed
light may instead result in
depression, despair, and uncertainty.

As with the passing of the
moon ending the eclipse,
our light may too shine
brightly once more as well.
To speed its passing, listen to the
quiet messages within, in between
your racing thoughts, then follow
                       the loving messages you hear.

Another Choice

Humanity chooses to live
in a world of inequity,
prejudice, injustice.
Their choice is predicated
on accepting the self-
centered beliefs they were
brought up to believe were
normal; they are not.
These tenets are the underlying
cause of many of humanity's
problems and challenges in life.

There is another choice though;
one that will challenge all of
our fundamental convictions.
We may instead treat all others
with kindness, compassion,
and love, selflessly sharing
our excess and inherent
goodness with all in need.
This will not only bring
meaning to our lives,
but also further the
spiritual evolution of
our planet as well.

The Distraction

Much of what we experience
in life is simply a distraction,
meant to occupy us as we
waste our lives foolishly
pursuing the false dreams
of success and happiness
we learned about when
we were young.

Nothing we are taught
though, or is found in the
self-centered world, will
allow us to find either
genuine success or happiness.

To truly live a successful
happy life, we must first
embrace the messages of
our spirit, present within
every life, then selflessly
share its inherent wisdom
and unconditional love,
without benefit or motive,
to help others realize this
is what they are meant
to do as well.

Dying of the Light

We are born with a
blinding light shining
so brightly darkness
cannot penetrate it.
From our first breath though,
our light begins to dim,
as we are taught to accept
the self-centered beliefs
of the world.
The more we believe what
we are taught, the dimmer
our light becomes.

As our light further loses its
luster, some may become
stressed, depressed, anxious,
struggling to find happiness,
inner peace, and love, in a
world these may never
be found in.

To rediscover our light,
it is necessary to abandon
the false self-centered beliefs
we once blindly accepted as
true, embracing, instead, the
inherent wisdom of unconditional
loving beliefs of the
spirit, our light, within.

The Spirit Within

A homeless, unknown
person is not as important
as a wealthy, famous one.
An animal, tree, or any
other form of life is not as
important as a human being.
An uneducated person is
not as important as a
highly educated one.
A janitor is not as
important as a president.

Every one of these
statements is untrue.
Every life, regardless of
our differences,
accomplishments, or
genus, has a spirit, a
piece of god within.
Each life, therefore, is,
and has always been
equally important.

Inequality

How do we justify inequality?
Depending on where you
were born, your upbringing,
the color of your skin, your
ability to get a good education,
or any number of other
differences, many struggle
daily to survive, while others
have the best life offers.

Accepting this paradigm
is the cause of greed,
prejudice, inequity.
It is also the underlying
cause of homelessness,
war, hunger, and numerous
other challenges experienced
by so many in the world.

Only when all our resources
are equally shared and our
belief in entitlement challenged,
may these problems finally
be addressed, and the spiritual
evolution of humanity truly begin.

Controlling Our Ego

The ego is everything we
learn, believe, and accept
is true after we are born.
Its only concern is for what
is best for us; it worries
little for any others.
For many, the ego makes
most or all of their life
decisions, as they
thoughtlessly follow its
self-centered directions,
believing everything
they were taught.

Though the ego will always
be a part of our lives, it need
not dominate our choices,
nor was it ever meant to.
Humanity was always
supposed to primarily follow
the guidance of the spirit,
a piece of god present
within every life.

The spirit's purpose is
to share its innate wisdom
and unconditional love to
help guide our life's choices.

With the acceptance of
the spiritual path, the ego
surrenders its control of
our life, allowing us to
begin a quest to discover
the genuine reason
for our life's journey.

Why Are We Born?

Are we born to get a
good job, make a lot of
money, have a family,
buy material possessions,
enjoy the best things
life has to offer?
Or is there another reason?
When we die, our bodies
will be buried or cremated.
Nothing we accumulated or
accomplished in our life
will accompany us.

Though our spirit may live
on in the heart and memories
of some we met, can we
say we discovered the
genuine reason for our birth?
Nothing listed above
will answer that question.

The reason we are born is
to reunite with our spirit
within, then selflessly share
its inherent wisdom and
unconditional love with all
others, so they too will
be able to remember their
genuine purpose in life as well.

What is Truth?

Truth is a belief something is right.
The question is: where did
that belief come from?
We begin to learn the truth
when we are children as we
are taught what to believe
and how to survive in a
self-centered world.
When we accept these ideas,
we convince ourselves
this is what the truth is.

There are some things
we learn that are true,
especially when the facts
are backed up by science.
There are many others though,
we have accepted as the
truth that simply are not.
Some believe they are better
than another due to their
superior education, job, race,
religion, wealth, sex, or any
number of other differences.
This belief is the underlying
cause of many of humanity's
problems seen throughout
our very divided world.

The truth is we are all
equal, important, *despite*
our many differences or
accomplishments in life.
Each life, has a spirit, a
piece of god within,
inextricably connecting
each of us to the other.
No one life, therefore, is,
or ever has been better,
more important than
then another's.

The Fog of Life

It is drizzling, rain passing
through a thick fog,
disguising everything
surrounding it.
Beneath the fog, we walk
carefully, trying not to get wet.
We hide under an umbrella,
perhaps a doorway, waiting
for the rain to end.

Many of us go through life
in a fog, trying to avoid the
hurdles placed in front of us.
We struggle to avoid the rain
and fog, hiding from life,
accepting the illusions
we learned are true.
It is only by walking through
the rain and dense fog though,
not hiding in the doorways
and accepting everything we
thought was true, life may
finally be understood.

Once the fog of life evaporates,
all that is left is the spirit, a
piece of god present to give
our lives meaning by sharing

its inherent wisdom and
unconditional love to help
guide our life's choices.

Only then may a true
understanding about life
emerge, as the many false
illusions we learned as
children are finally recognized.

Our Aura

Others may observe much
about us by the aura
we radiate to the world.
For many, stress, or any
number of other daily
challenges in life, darken
the subtle non-verbal
messages we each emit.

The more we believe what
we learned about how to
survive and succeed in a
self-centered world, the
darker our aura becomes.

To lighten our aura, lessen
our stresses, and begin a
journey to discover our
true purpose in life, sit quietly,
listen intently to the silence
in between your racing
thoughts, then embrace the
wisdom and tender loving
messages you hear within.

The Balcony

Looking down from the
balcony we see a world
in disarray; one where
distrust, fear, and endless
struggle manifest.
Hate, prejudice, make some
believe they are more
deserving than others;
they are not.

Living in a self-centered
world, focusing only on
what is best for ourself,
is the cause of these beliefs
and many of humanity's
challenges in life.

Only when we accept
everyone, regardless of
our differences, is equal,
important, and deserving,
will our view from above
change, seeing instead a
world of equity, compassion,
and universal love.

Priorities

The resources of our
planet are exploited by
the wealthy, for the
benefit of the few.
Humanity spends incredible
amounts of money preparing
or fighting wars, rather than
spending this money to
help those most in need.

They buy bombs and
bullets to kill people,
rather than food for the
hungry or to provide
shelter for the homeless.
This is insanity, solved only
by a paradigm shift; one that
requires putting the needs
of all before those of
the privileged few.

Happiness

Wishing to be happy,
some buy nice things,
have a family, try
to enjoy life.
This type of happiness
though, is fleeting, lasting
only until changes in our
life circumstances
end our bliss.

To find true everlasting
happiness, we must first
reunite with our spirit within,
then selflessly share its
wisdom and unconditional
love with all others.
Only when we help others
discover their happiness
as well, may we truly
discover what happiness is.
.

Darkness and Light

Darkness results from
embracing certain beliefs
we learn when we are young.
These beliefs then dominate
our lives, as we react to
the world around us.
We learn to be self-centered,
untrusting, fearful of
being hurt by others.

We may become indifferent
to the prejudice, inequity,
and struggles of others,
as we try to survive in a
harsh, often cruel world.
Our guardrails not only
shield us from harm,
but also isolate us from
others as well, hiding our
light from the world.

Light radiates from
embracing our spirit,
a piece of god present
within every life, there to
share its wisdom and
unconditional love to help
guide our life choices.

We each have a choice
which to follow:
darkness or light.
To discover life's true
purpose, choose the path
of light, then selflessly
share your light
with the world.

Our Journey Through Life

With our birth, from our
first breath, we learn how
to act, what to believe,
how to survive in a
self-centered world.
Though some of what we
learn is necessary, many
go through their entire
life never questioning
if these beliefs are true.

As we get older, some
may begin to wonder if
they really are true.
There is an uncertainty,
unrest within, telling
them it may not be.
With time, as we start to
confront the many untruths
we learned when we were
young, understanding few
of them were true, we begin
to realize we spent our entire
lives pursuing an illusion.

With the complete embrace
of the spiritual path, we find
the answers we have sought.

Selflessly sharing our spirit's wisdom and unconditional love with others, we will also discover our true purpose in life as well.

Human vs Spiritual Plane

We each exist, simultaneously,
on two planes of existence.
One is the human plane.
On this plane, we follow the
self-centered rules of society.
We judge others using the
matrix we learned as
we were growing up.

The spiritual plane is
quite different though.
Within every life is a spirit,
a piece of god present to
share its innate wisdom
and unconditional love,
so all may discover the
spiritual plane in
their life as well.

Though both the human and
spiritual plane exist at the
same time, they are often
in conflict with each other.
Only one will lead to true
understanding; the other
to a life without
purpose or meaning.
Only by embracing the

spiritual plane through life,
may we discover the genuine
reason for our life's journey.

The Virus

We are healthy when we are born.
Almost immediately, a
virus affecting our overall
health is created infecting
every cell in our body,
lasting, for some,
their entire life.

This virus is the ego, our
learned beliefs; it will be
with us until we die.
It teaches us how to survive
in a self-centered world of
fear and distrust, being
concerned only for our
well-being, with little
concern for any others.

This virus may only begin
to be treated by embracing
the selfless messages of the
spirit within, then following
its wisdom and loving
guidance as our primary
guide in life.

The Cost of Enlightenment

Enlightenment is completely
accepting the path of the
spirit within as our primary
guide in life, rather than
blindly following the
path of the ego, our
self-centered beliefs.
Challenging the status quo,
everything we were taught
and accepted as true,
changes your life forever.

Achieving enlightenment
though, is very difficult
and expensive.
Absolutely nothing in your
life will ever be the same again.
Once your journey begins it
may not be reversed.
Your job, marriage, friendships,
how you view the world, are
just a few of the many
things that may change.

Though few will actually
become enlightened in their
lifetime, the unending journey
will continue until we die.

Enlightenment will lead to
a life of meaning, purpose,
and understanding.
We each must decide for
ourself, if the cost is too great.

How Long?

So much hate, fear,
prejudice; so many
needless deaths,
hungry, homeless.
How long will we
allow this to continue?

We are taught we cannot
change the struggles
so many endure.
This is a lie, fabricated
by a self-centered society
to convince us to
accept the status quo.

We must each challenge
this myth, embracing
courage instead of fear,
acceptance instead of
prejudice, and love
instead of hate.

The Eyes of a Child

When a young child sees
the world, their view is
not yet skewed by the
dictates and traditions
of the world.
They see a world of
endless possibilities,
one where there is hope,
love, and compassion.
They have not yet learned
to be cynical, prejudiced, uncaring.

As they begin to get older
though, they become fearful,
as they are taught to accept
the mores of society.
Their innocence, once pure,
has begun to fade, causing
them to forget the path
through life they were
meant to pursue.
Instead, they follow the
self-centered illusional path
they were told would bring
them success and happiness.

To change the direction of
the world, save our planet

from humanity's destructive tendencies, we all need to remember and embrace the world as it could be, when we first looked at it through the eyes of a young child.

A Glimmer of Light

When we are born,
our light illuminates
the entire world.
From that first moment
though, its brightness
begins to dull as we are
taught how to survive in a
self-centered harsh world.
Despite our upbringing and
challenges in life though,
within every life lingers
a glimmer of light.

For some who have
accepted most of the
messages they learned,
this light is quite dusky.
For others it glows more
brightly, as the original
memory of our spirit within,
still has some influence
on their daily choices.

It is not too late to change
the direction of our life.
By embracing and accepting the
wisdom and unconditional loving
messages of our spirit, once

unimpeded by our learned illusions of life, our light may once again reemerge and shine brightly, as it was always meant to do.

Follow Your Heart

When we make decisions
in life, do we follow our
loving heart, or are our
decisions based on
what we learned?
Though there are occasions
these are the same, many
times the choices we make
would be quite different
depending on which
we are listening to.

The ego, our self-centered
beliefs, only considers
what is best for itself.
The spirit, however, not
only considers this, but
also is concerned for
what is best for everyone
else as well.

To find inner peace,
happiness, love, and
genuine meaning in
life, always follow
your heart.

Walk With Humility

When we do or say
something, do we
expect a reward?
Is it something we do
to improve our self-esteem,
to impress others, or are our
actions shared whole-heartedly?

It is only when we walk
through life with humility,
the true essence of life
will reveal itself.

Listen

Listen intently to what others say.

Hear the genuine meaning
underneath the layers of
protection, the façade we
erect to shield ourselves
from the judgment of others.

See past the superficial
words disguising the
genuine message.
Only then will we truly
know another's thoughts.

It's All Noise

The world is loud,
chaotic, unforgiving.
Distractions constantly
challenge us, making us
fearful, untrusting, causing
us to withdraw into a
cocoon to protect ourselves.
Living our life encased in
a bubble, endorsing the
narrative we were taught,
leads to a life of mediocrity.

It is only when we understand
this is all a distraction,
diverting us from our true
purpose, accepting and
embracing the wisdom and
quiet unconditional loving
messages of our spirit within,
that life's true intention
may be realized.

Our Internal Struggle

Many spend their lives
unraveling the emotional
damage done when
they were children.
This injury results from
teaching our children to
accept the many false
misleading opinions about
how to survive in
a self-centered world.

Though some of these
beliefs are necessary to
help us live in society,
it is those encouraging
the egoistic devotion
to only ourselves,
that is the root cause
of our lifelong pain.

To undo the damage, we
must confront the baseless
lies and beliefs we learned
about when we were young,
embracing instead, the
loving selfless beliefs
of our spirit within.

Our Harmful Emotions

All harmful emotions result
from living in a self-centered
world, accepting the many
falsehoods we learn, as
we are taught how to
conform to society's rules.
Though some of these
guidelines are necessary,
most others encourage
the negative behaviors
destroying our planet
and the lives of so many.

Every harmful trait and
emotion is learned; they do
not exist before we are born.
To eliminate evil, hate,
prejudice, and all other
destructive beliefs and
behaviors, we must expand
our focus from solely worrying
only about ourselves, to
include selflessly caring
for the well-being of every
life on our planet as well.

The Source

After we are born, we
are taught to accept the
many false self-centered
beliefs of the world.

Our purpose in life is to
return to the peaceful bliss
we once knew, before our
birth, by embracing and
selflessly sharing the inherent
wisdom and pure untainted
love of our spirit within.

Captives in Life

Many live their entire
life in captivity.
It is a prison they have
created themselves by
accepting the dictates
and beliefs of humanity.
Though they may be
successful, enjoy the best
life offers, they remain
imprisoned, living in an
insensitive self-centered
world, believing they
are free; they are not.

To open the prison door,
escape its confines, they
must first reexamine their
definition of success.
Success truly has little to do
with our accomplishments
in the world.

True success may only be
found by embracing the
inherent wisdom and
unconditional loving
messages of our spirit
within, then selflessly
sharing them with all others.

Accept the Message You Hear

We may each change
the world by listening
to the quiet voice within,
accepting its innate wisdom
and message of unconditional
love, then selflessly sharing
it to encourage others to
hear this message as well.

This is Enlightenment

Within every sentient life,
regardless of accomplishments,
differences, or genus, lies
god, spirit, soul, intimately
connecting each to the other.

Though we are all unique,
since every life has a piece
of god within, each life
is equally important.

Understanding this is
enlightenment.

The Darkness Behind Our Smile

To the entire world,
we appear blessed.
We have a good job,
family, home.
Our constant smile
convinces the world of our
happiness and accomplishments.
Yet behind the smile, the facade
we learned long ago to present
to the world, lies a broken,
unhappy, stressed, person.
We became so good protecting
ourself from those who would
abuse us, we developed an
alter ego, one that masked
our internal struggle, allowing
us to survive in a harsh,
judgmental world.

Though we project an image
of a happy successful
person, nothing could
be further from the truth.
Some of us have developed
coping mechanisms, using
drugs or drinking alcohol to
bury their true emotions and feelings.

To confront our darkness,
we must first look within.
Only by embracing and
sharing the inherent wisdom
and unconditional love of our
spirit, realizing our genuine
worth and importance does
not lie in the self-centered
world, but by selflessly
sharing our spirit's wisdom
and love with others, may
our darkness lighten,
beginning us on a journey
to discover the genuine
meaning of life.

Apathy

Surrendering to the status
quo, we blindly accept the
many flaws and lies we learn
about and believe to be true.
Many become apathetic,
believing there is little they
can do to improve the hardships
experienced by so many.

Though some may attempt to
make changes, these are often
temporary, as the underlying
problems causing these
difficulties have not
yet been addressed.

Until humanity genuinely
understands every life's true
worth, regardless of their
accomplishments, differences,
or genus, embracing the ideas
of equality, selflessness, and
sharing our excess to help all
others, apathy will continue,
further leading to the
deterioration and extinction
of more forms of life
on our very fragile planet.

Death

The end of life is a
fascinating period of time.
Though we may have ideas
about what happens after we
die, from philosophers, religion,
books we have read, our
imagination, we truly do not know.

What some believe is our body,
which houses our spirit within,
will cease to exist, allowing
our immortal spirit to return
to a higher plane of existence,
until it returns to join
with another sentient life.

Though with our physical
death our body and ego,
our self-centered beliefs,
will cease to exist, a part of
our spirit will also continue
to influence and live on in
all those who we had met
and selflessly helped during
our brief journey through life.

From Pain to Wisdom

When we are young,
learning life's guidelines,
struggling to survive in a
competitive often harsh,
self-centered world, we
learn how to protect ourselves
from the verbal slings and
arrows others use to prove
their dominance and superiority.
We may easily get our feelings
hurt, as we internalize their words.

Though these events often
happened when we were
young, they may continue
to haunt us when we are older.
Those who start their spiritual
journey though, are able to
begin to see past the pain and
cruel words that once were spoken.

With age and spiritual
growth comes wisdom.
And with wisdom, the ability
to see beyond the egoistic words
that caused us so much pain
throughout our life, allowing
us to see now only the pure
loving messages within.

Our Words

The words we speak
may spread love, but
also may be the cause
of significant pain.
Sincere encouraging loving
words may help ease another's
journey through life, improving
their positive view of
themself and of life itself.

Negative hurtful words though,
may remain and have harmful
effects on someone for
the rest of their life.
Even one encounter
may help or harm someone.

Let us therefore strive to
truly support others by
sincerely being caring,
compassionate, and loving,
always speaking with
kindness, rather than malice.

Helping All in Need

A majority of the world
accepts the man-made
limitations we have
imposed on ourself.
By embracing the status
quo, we allow life to
impose its will on us.
We believe there is little
we may do to improve the
quality of life for those
most in need: the homeless,
hungry, survivors of war,
and so many others facing
life's daily challenges.

In reality, we were all
deceived to accept this truth.
It is time for us to impose our
collective will on life,
challenging this fallacy.

By embracing our spirit's
wisdom and unconditional
loving guidance, we may
help all those deprived of
their most basic needs,
equally sharing the resources
of our planet, and selflessly

promoting peace, compassion
and love, for all those who
are struggling and in need of help.

We Are All Children of the World

We live is a very divided
world, separated by religion,
country, sex, wealth, race,
and other ways too numerous
to mention, justifying our
harmful beliefs and
actions toward others.
These differences are used
to rationalize war, hate,
prejudice, inequity.

Our dysfunctional world is
slowly falling into an abyss,
descending toward
its bottomless crater.
We must realize we are
all children of the world,
related by a common purpose
and spark of the divine
present within each.

Only by embracing love,
compassion, and equality,
helping all in need without
alternative intentions, may
the direction and future
of our world evolve,
allowing our planet and
all life on it to thrive.

Every Life is Sentient

Regardless if life is
human, animal, or any
other form of life existing
in the vast universe, every
life, each with a spark of
the divine present within,
is equally valuable.

Though mankind is the
dominant species on our
planet, it does not mean
our life is more significant
than another's or
another form of life.

Everything alive has a right
to exist, its life to be respected,
and given an opportunity to
discover its genuine purpose in life.

The Cure

To find our light within
we must first confront
our darkness.
Though our life begins
in light, darkness starts
immediately after we are
born as we are socialized
and exposed to the many
beliefs and influences of
the world around us.

To challenge darkness, and
rediscover our light, we
must realize it was our
acceptance of society's
self-centered beliefs that
was its cause.

The cure: truly
understanding this by
fully embracing and
selflessly sharing our
light's inherent wisdom
and unconditional love
to help others rediscover
their light within as well.

Judging Each Other

When we see another,
we often decide what
we think of them.
We see their race, appearance,
sex, and many other things
we learned differentiate
us from each other.
Even before they speak,
we often have formed
an opinion about them.

Though we do not
understand the challenges
they have had in their life,
or their beauty and love
existing within, we have
already decided if we
wish to spend time
getting to know them.

Every person, every life,
each with a spirit, a
piece of god within,
is a gift to all.
We are blessed to be
given the opportunity
to share in everyone's
passage through life.

Regardless of our
differences, we must
embrace each other,
without reservation
or judgment, selflessly
sharing our wisdom, love,
and essence, with every person.
Only then will life's true
purpose become evident.

Compassion, Love, and Humanity

We have always lived in
a very troubled world;
one where self-preservation
directs our beliefs,
thoughts, and actions.
We have therefore neglected
the needs of others, struggling
to survive in an indifferent world.

When we were young, before
we were exposed to the dictates
of the world, we once possessed
compassion and love.
With our socialization and
concern for only ourselves
and success in life though,
we lost our humanity.

To rediscover it, we must try
to remember what we once knew:
to selflessly share our compassion,
love, and humanity with all others,
without reservation, to help others
rediscover their compassion,
love and humanity as well.
Only then may our humanity
be restored, allowing each of
us to discover our true
purpose in life as well.

The Lessons We are Born to Learn

Every life, not only on
our planet, but throughout
the vast universe, is inextricably
connected to each other by
a spirit, a piece of god
present within each.
It matters not our genus,
differences, or accomplishments,
our essence within unites
us all in a common journey.

Only when we truly understand
this, respecting the rights of
every sentient life, will our
life's purpose be discovered
and the lessons we are born
to learn be genuinely understood.

Forgiveness

When we harm another
in any manner, we may
cause them enduring pain.
It matters not if the injury is
emotional, physical, verbal,
or in any other form.
The hurt we caused is always
wrong, requiring pardon
to the one we injured.
Though we may believe we
are justified in our actions,
they never are.

Do not let our imperfect
humanity, our ego, allow
the wrong to happen or for
us not to sincerely apologize
if it has already occurred.
Only by correcting our
human indiscretions, will
we be able to awaken,
allowing us to begin a
quest to discover our
true purpose in life.

Why are We Born?

We are born to
live a life full of
love, freely shared
with all others.

By embracing the
inherent wisdom of our
spirit within, selflessly
sharing our unconditional
love for the good and benefit
of every life, we are fulfilling
our true destiny, the reason
for our life's journey.

How Do You Know You Are Awake?

Instead of seeing only
the worse in people, you
will now begin to see
the good instead.

Instead of darkness,
you will see light,
instead of helplessness,
you will want to selflessly
help others, and instead of
accepting living in a world
of fear, you will want to help
change the world so others
may live in a world of love instead.

Trusting Each Other

Living in a volatile
world of distrust, where
worry for ourselves is
more important than
concern for others, many
are cautious, afraid of
the many life challenges
that may inflict pain or loss.
They therefore are guarded,
untrusting of others.

Though caution may be
necessary, it will not be
until we sincerely begin
to consider the best interests
of all others that we may
truly begin to trust one
another and, in doing
so, improve life for all.

We Are All Related

Every life is intimately
linked, connected by a
spark of the divine,
present within each.

Only when humanity
truly recognizes this,
selflessly helping each
other, and treating each
life, regardless of our
differences or genus,
with respect, understanding,
and unconditional love,
may we understand
our life's true purpose.

Our Children May Change the World

The first five years of
every child's life is
the most important.
It is during this time they
learn what is expected
of them and how they
will react to different
situations in the world.
It is also when they will
develop an overall view of
humanity and how to treat others.

Their opinions, prejudices,
beliefs, and aspirations, often
begin during these early
formative years, and will
form the basis of how they
will act and think about
others, often for the
rest of their life.

Let us therefore raise our
children during these years
to treat everyone with love,
respect, and empathy,
understanding every life,
regardless of our differences,
is equally deserving.

We Must Not Remain Apathetic

How does a civilized society
allow any child or person to
die from starvation, senseless
violence, or a curable disease?
We become immune to the
horrors and impact of hate,
prejudice, and inequity.
Instead, these harmful
emotions become internalized,
a part of our DNA, as we
observe these things happen
every day around the world.

Every person can effect
change, though most believe
there is little they can do.
By sharing our truth, our
essence's inherent wisdom
and unconditional love, with
all others, regardless of our
many differences, we may
each positively alter the
direction and future of the world.

It is time to end our apathy,
our indifference, by selflessly
helping all others, ending the
needless hardships and struggles
experienced by so many.

Life

Every life, including people,
animals, plants, and all
other forms of life
throughout the universe,
is inextricably connected,
each having a spirit, a
piece of god within,
to guide its life, and
give it meaning.

No one life, therefore,
regardless of our differences,
accomplishments, or genus,
is, or ever has been, better or
more important than another's.

The Truth Translator

Life is so confusing, we
need an interpreter to
inform us what is true.
There often are many different
opinions about the same issue,
only dividing us further,
as we each seek clarity.
Our views regarding life are
influenced by our upbringing
and experiences in a
self-centered world.

Though we may believe we
know what is true, in actuality,
little of what we were taught,
absent scientific fact, is genuine.
It is a fantasy, created by
our learned beliefs, the ego.

To know the real truth,
we must learn to ignore
all the external noise, instead
permitting the quiet voice,
present within every life,
with its inherent wisdom
and messages of unconditional
love, to be heard.

The Price of Life

How much life costs has
absolutely nothing to do
with money or wealth.
Most believe it does though,
striving to obtain it, even if
it is at the cost of taking
advantage of others.
The results of living in
such a self-centered world
are war, hunger, envy,
prejudice, and many of
humanity's other self-
inflicted challenges in life.

One need not have riches
or material possessions
to live a successful life.
Rather, they merely must
embrace the wisdom and
soft unconditional loving
messages within, then
selflessly share them
with all others.

Those who are able to do
so, experience riches beyond
compare; for they are
rewarded with inner peace,

discover genuine meaning,
and will find authentic
love in their life as well.

The Ostrich

There is a myth an ostrich
will bury its head in the
sand when it is afraid.
The same may be said about
humanity, though with fear,
we genuinely do so, many
disregarding the realities
presented to us every day.

The list of man-made
fears is endless.
The threat of nuclear war,
climate change, prejudice,
poverty, are just a few of
the numerous things we
ignore believing there is
little we may do to alter
our destiny, or help those
who are struggling.

If we do nothing, continuing
to ignore the truth by burying
our head in the sand, our
fears may well become reality.

To change this paradigm,
allowing our children a
genuine chance to experience

life as it was meant to be,
we must all lift our head to
clearly see the danger
threatening us, and confront
it with courage, determination,
and unconditional love.

We Must Not Fail

Humanity has evolved,
discovering innovations
making life easier to
do laborious tasks.
Inventions and scientific
knowledge has furthered
man's dominance over our planet.

Our growth, however,
has been mostly limited to
the world in which we exist.
It only modestly includes the
spiritual evolution of our species.

Without the inclusion of our
spirit's inherent wisdom and
sharing its unconditional
love to help others, though
our lives may be easier,
humanity is destined to fail.

One Truth

Though each of us have
our own self-centered
opinions and views about
life, in reality, there is but
one underlying truth, uniting
us and all other forms of life together.

We are inextricably linked
to each other by a spirit, a piece
of god present to give our lives
meaning by sharing its inherent
wisdom and unconditional love
to help guide our life's choices.

Without this understanding,
though we may have lived a
successful life if our success
was not shared with others,
it will have been lived
without consequence.

Only by embracing our
universal bond, sincerely
recognizing the importance
of every life, will life's true
meaning become apparent.

Power

As we are taught to accept
society's norms and beliefs,
we learn power is obtained
from wealth, a commanding
job, our dominance over others.

This view of life though,
presenting the appearance
of power, is an illusion,
created by the ego, our
learned beliefs, to distract us
from our true source of strength.

Genuine power may not be
found in the self-centered world.
Money, prestige, control over
others, will not satisfy this urge.
True power must first be
found within, then selflessly
shared, without motive or
benefit, with all others.

Echoes in Life

There is so much noise
and chaos in the world, it
inhibits the quiet messages
of our spirit within.
Though we may sense its
presence, it appears as an echo,
its voice muffled in the distance,
preventing us from clearly
learning from its innate wisdom.

For those who begin to question
all they were taught about life,
the chaos and loudness of
the world begins to lessen.
Everything we learned and
believed to be true is the
cause of our turmoil
and commotion.

When we genuinely
understand little we were
taught was true, the world
will become silent, as the
echoes in our life
finally disappear.

Every Life is Valuable

Every life, regardless of our
differences or accomplishments,
is equally important, each
worthy of empathy, respect,
and unconditional love.

Though our experiences and
personalities are different,
inherent within each of us
is a spirit, a piece of god,
intimately connecting
us to each other.

Only by embracing this
common bond, may we
truly begin to understand
our reason for being.

A Human Issue

Our thoughts, beliefs, and
experiences, help form
the person we become.
Combined, they influence
our path through life as
we embrace prejudice,
inequity, indifference to
the struggles of others,
as a normal part of life.

The one commonality
found in each, is that
they are created after
we are born, as we learn
what is expected of us to
survive and succeed in an
often cruel, competitive
self-centered world.

Though it is important
we understand these
things, it is our blind
obedience to them
that is the cause of
many of humanity's
self-inflicted challenges.

Only when we genuinely

realize these self-centered
beliefs hide our true purpose
in life, to selflessly share
our inherent wisdom and
unconditional love, our
spirit, with all others,
will life's many challenges
lessen, allowing the true
reason for our life's
journey to be revealed.

We Are All Brothers and Sisters

We are brought up to
believe those we have not
met, strangers, are not
important, because we are
not related or know them.
Humanity therefore ignores
these individuals, each instead
worrying only about themselves
and those closest to them.

This self-centered belief is
the reason for many of
humanity's challenges and
inequities, as the world
accepts this as its reality.
In actuality, there are no strangers.
Everyone is related by a common
purpose and connection.

We are all brothers and sisters,
intimately linked by a spirit,
a piece of god present
within each of us.
Only together, selflessly
sharing our spirit's wisdom
and unconditional love to help
each other, may we all flourish.

Apart, our life will have been
lived without meaning, as
we will have totally accepted
the isolating self-centered
illusions we first learned
when we were young.

The Essence of Life

After we are born, we are
taught what is important,
the essence of life.
We learn about the
expectations of the world
and to worry only about our
own success and happiness.

Though success may
make our lives easier,
it is how it is achieved
and the belief it need
not be shared, that is the
reason for many of the
needless struggles in the world.

It is an illusion success
and true happiness may
be found in a self-centered
world; they may not.
If our success is not selflessly
shared with others, though we
may believe we are successful
and happy, in truth, we
will know neither,

Human Capacity

Human beings have
demonstrated an enormous
ability to learn as they
invent technology to make
their lives easier.
They are also beginning to
understand not only the earth
on which we live, but the
very origins of the
universe itself as well.

With this ability, some
have become protective,
greedy, self-centered.
In their desire to live an
affluent life, they have forgotten,
neglected the most important part
of our existence, our spiritual capacity.
Though organized religion
began with noble intentions
attempting to address this, its
ideas long ago were transformed
by human interpretations of
divine concepts and beliefs.

Without spiritual insight,
though our lives may have
been successful, they will

have been lived without
purpose or meaning, completely
disregarding the authentic
reason for our life's journey:
to selflessly share our spirit's
wisdom and unconditional
love with others, so all may
live a successful life as well.

In Darkness, See the Light

Within every life, there
is both darkness and light.
Darkness represents our
acquired values, accepted
without hesitation, as we
are taught about the self-
centered world into
which we are born.
These beliefs are the
cause of many of humanity's
struggles, negative attitudes,
and harmful ideologies
they believe are normal;
they are not.

Within each of us
though, is also light.
Light symbolizes our
original purpose, forgotten,
suppressed by our
learned egoistic beliefs.
Spirit is inherent within
every life, giving each
life purpose and meaning.

It is a choice which we
believe and will follow:
darkness or light.

We may alter our
path at any time.
Though darkness will
always remain with us,
choose to allow light
to be your primary
guide in life.
With this choice, not
only will your spirit shine
brighter, but the genuine
reason for your life's
journey will be
realized as well.

Our Essence

There is an essence
within every life, present
to give our lives meaning
by sharing its wisdom and
unconditional love to help
guide our life's choices.

It is our purpose in life to
recognize, accept, and selflessly
share our essence's wisdom
and love with all others, so
they too may rediscover their
essence within as well.

Mental Illness

Beyond the known causes
of mental illness, lie a deeper,
more fundamental source.
It concerns the conflict
between the ego, our
self-centered beliefs,
and the spirit, a piece
of god accompanying
each life to be our guide
by sharing its inherent
wisdom and unconditional love.

Following our spirit's
guidance and selflessly
sharing it with others is
the genuine purpose
of our life's journey.
The ego and spirit are
like siblings, constantly
arguing, each attempting
to get us to follow their
direction and beliefs.

Their views about life though,
are diametrically opposite.
The ego is concerned only
for self-gratification and what
is best for us; the spirit,

however, is also concerned
about helping all others as well.
This unresolved tension is an
underlying cause of many
mental illnesses, as well as
unresolved stress and anxiety.

Though both will remain
with us throughout our
lives, by only treating the
mind and body, therapy
will result in partial resolution.
Only by including the spirit as
part of any treatment may these
illnesses be fully treated and
may someone, not only be
able to function in the
world, but also discover
true happiness, love, and
meaning in their life as well.

Our Self

Though human beings are
extraordinarily complex,
in actuality, they are a
combination of just two
separate elements; each
is necessary for survival.

Many struggle, embracing
primarily the human self,
our self-centered beliefs.
This part of our self is
concerned only for what
is best for us; it is the
cause of many of humanity's
problems and needless
challenges in the world.

The other part of the self
is the spirit, a piece of god
present within each life.
Its purpose is to guide
our life's choices by
sharing its wisdom and
unconditional love.
Following our spirit's
guidance will allow
us to find true love,
happiness, inner peace,

and meaning in our life.

We each may choose
which to follow.
One will lead to the
continuation and further
decline of humanity.
The other to the advancement
and evolution of our species.
Unless a choice is made soon,
one may be made for us.

We Are One People

It matters not our appearance,
skin color, religion, ethnicity,
or any other differences
there are between us.
Wealth, fame, prestige,
have little meaning as well.

We are one people, intimately
linked by a spirit, a piece of
god present within each.
We are alive to selflessly
help each other by sharing
our spirit's inherent wisdom
and unconditional love,
for the benefit of all.

The Battle for Supremacy

A conflict has been
raging within each
of us since humanity
first appeared on our planet.
On one side of the conflict is
the ego, our self-centered beliefs.
On the other side lies the spirit,
present within every life
to give our life purpose.

To understand the result
of living in a world where
the ego is dominate, simply
look at the many needless
challenges, too numerous to
list, resulting from its supremacy.

The earth is at an inflection point.
If we do not choose to support
the spirit in this battle, it is our
children, all life on our planet,
and our planet itself that will
suffer the consequences.

What Really Matters?

What is important?
Is it success, wealth, family,
material possessions, or is
there more to life than
our own desires?
Though these and other
things make our lives easier,
they will not aid us in
discovering our life's true purpose.

Safety, sustenance, shelter,
are necessary for survival.
Most other things though,
we desire so our life will be
easier and more enjoyable.

To discover life's meaning,
find genuine happiness,
inner peace, and true love,
after we have secured our
basic needs, we must then
selflessly share our excess
with those less fortunate,
helping each secure their
basic needs as well.

How Can I Help?

There are so many
hardships experienced by
countless people throughout
the world, it is overwhelming
to know where to begin to
try to aid others in need.
We therefore may believe
there is little we can do to
improve the lives of those
who are struggling.

This belief, encouraged by
our acceptance of the self-
centered status quo, is untrue.
Every person may change the world.

To do so, we must open our
heart, embrace the wisdom
and unconditional loving
messages we hear, then share
them, without hesitation
or cause, with all others.

The Evolution of Humanity

With the advent of
the human race, their
intelligence permitted
them to become the
dominant species on our planet.
Though their intellect allowed
them to discover and invent
many things to help make
our lives easier, and our
knowledge of our planet
and the universe more
understandable, humanity's
spiritual evolution remains
in its infancy.

Though there have been
noble attempts by different
religions to understand
the importance of spirituality,
organized religions eventually
adopted man's self-centered
interpretation of god, diluting
the original messages and
meaning of love, compassion,
and concern for all, they
were meant to convey.

Humanity is at a crossroads.

If they continue on their
current path, ignoring the
many hardships of others
and our planet, their
evolutionary cycle, as
so many others, may be
complete; humanity will
become a distant memory,
remembered by the skeletal
remains of their intelligence.

To prevent this potential
outcome, humanity must
selflessly help each other by
embracing our genuine spiritual
nature, present within every life,
always considering first what
is for everyone, all life, and
our planet itself, before only
worrying about what
is best for themselves.

An Alternate Reality

Living in a self-centered
world, we are alone, worrying
only about our own survival.
Money, prestige, fame, material
possessions, dictate success,
triggering the inequities
and struggles of so many
around the world.

Life need not be this way.
We may choose instead to
live our life with love, rather
than fear, by selflessly helping
others, for the benefit of all.

The First Step to Awakening

Awakening begins when
we question if there may
be more to life than just
becoming successful.
Despite doing all the things
we were taught would make
our lives happy, important,
and meaningful, a feeling
begins to emerge within,
that something is wrong.
Though we may have money,
fame, and many possessions,
this unrelenting sensation
will not stop.

We awaken when, despite
our best efforts to ignore it,
we no longer can, and must
begin to make changes in
our life that will forever
alter our path, as we
begin to question the truth
of all we had been taught.

A New Beginning

Life's challenges affect everyone.
While wealth and privilege
may make them easier, no
one may escape their
influence on our lives.
Though those struggling
for daily survival have
more trials, others often
confront fears haunting
them from years gone by.

It is possible to lessen
these burdens, almost
instantaneously, by viewing
life through a different prism.
For those who gaze at life
through spiritual eyes,
allowing their spirit, present
within every life to be their
primary guide, most challenges,
regardless of cause, lessen,
as the genuine realization of
life's meaning, to selflessly
share our wisdom, love,
compassion, and excess, with
all others, becomes clear.

With this understanding, our

life's journey starts anew,
as we begin on a newfound
path to share our spirit's
wisdom and unconditional
love with all others.

Life's True Purpose

Within every life, regardless
of form, is a spirit, a piece
of god present to guide our
lives with its inherent wisdom
and unconditional love
to help others in need.

Those who never realize
this, though they may
have led a successful life,
approach death without
knowing life's true purpose.
Others, who begin to question
what success is, sensing the
first messages from their
spirit within, awaken.

Once they genuinely realize
everything they were told
that would allow them to
live a successful life was
an illusion, they will experience
life as it was meant to be:
with inner peace, true joy,
authentic love, and
discover the genuine
meaning of life as well.

Money or Meaning

Though it is possible
to have both money
and meaning, many
forget the true reason
they were born with
their pursuit of the former.

Genuine meaning must
first be found within,
then selflessly shared
with others.

It may not be found by
itself in a self-centered
world, without first
embracing the wisdom
and unconditional love
of the spirit within.
Then, it may only be
realized, when it is shared,
without motive of benefit,
with all others.

Why Are We Alive?

Why are we alive?
There may come a time
in each of our lives we ask
ourselves this question.
For many, their answer is to
succeed, enjoying the many
opportunities life presents us.
To them, success is defined
by money, fame, prestige,
family, material possessions.

Though these things may make
our lives easier and more
enjoyable, none of them will
answer the question above.
Why are we alive?
We are alive to selflessly
share the inherent wisdom
and unconditional love of
our spirit, present within
every life, so others may also
answer this question, and
realize their life's
true purpose as well.

Success

Our life will only be
successful if we selflessly
help all others become
successful as well.
Though we may become
wealthy, be famous, have a
prestigious job, if our
success is does not benefit
others, our life will have
been lived without
purpose or meaning.

True success may not
be achieved in a self-
centered world or alone.
It may only be attained when
it is shared, without motive
or benefit, with all others.

We Are Alive to Help Each Other

It is never acceptable
to intentionally harm
another in any way.
It matters not the provocation,
or if the injury is verbal,
physical, emotional, or
in any other manner.

We are alive to support
each other through life's
many challenges.
Only together will we succeed.
Apart, though we may have
achieved much, we will have
overlooked the genuine
purpose for our life's journey.

Life's Genuine Purpose

The purpose of life is to
embrace and accept the
spiritual path, then selflessly
share it with others so they
too may realize this as well.

Anything else is a distraction,
meant to challenge our choices
in life, as we confront the many
diversions life presents us.

With the complete acceptance
of the spiritual path as our
primary guide in life, inner
peace and love surround our
entire being, as life's genuine
purpose becomes apparent.

The Deep State

We are born knowing
only unconditional love,
meant to be shared
freely, with all others.
Any other beliefs or
emotions, acquired after
our birth, may be defined
as the deep state, the cause
of many of humanity's ills.

To discover the genuine
reason for our life's journey,
we must return to the pure
state of love we once knew
before we learned, accepted,
and followed the path
of the deep state.

A Moment of Grace

Perhaps if we stop for
a moment, quiet our
minds, listen to the quiet
soothing loving messages
within, we may experience
a meaningful reflection,
an echo of a time before
we were exposed
to life's illusions.

What we would witness
is a world where our
directive is to genuinely
care, help, and love each
other, regardless of our
differences, by selflessly
sharing our spirit's
wisdom and unconditional
love to help all others.

This moment of grace is
reflective of our life's
true mission; it is the
reason we are born,
the meaning of life.

The Negotiator

Within each person,
there are two diametrically
polar opposite belief systems,
each competing for dominance.
Our experiences in life,
acceptance of societal
norms, among many
other factors, determine
which we will follow.
Present is a mediator to
help us decide the
right thing to do.

On one end of the
spectrum is the ego,
our self-centered beliefs.
Its only concern is what
is best for us; it worries
little about others.
On the other end of the
spectrum is the spirit, a
piece of god accompanying
each of us on our life's journey.
The spirit's concern is for
all, understanding we are
inextricably connected to
each other by its common
presence within us.

The negotiator helps decide
which belief system
takes precedence.
When these systems
are in balance or when
the ego is predominant,
the destructive nature of
humanity dominates
our decisions, resulting
in greed, prejudice,
inequity, and all of
humanity's harmful actions.

It is only when the spirit
is the primary guide in
our life that inner peace,
authentic love, and
meaning may embrace
our lives, as the genuine
purpose for our life's
journey is understood.

Inequality

We live in a world where
some believe their life is
more important than others.
Our world is endlessly
divided by wealth, race,
ethnicity, religion, and in
numerous other ways,
granting favor to some,
while causing others
to needlessly struggle.

The truth is absolutely
no one, regardless of
our many differences or
achievements in life,
is or ever has been
better than another.
Every life, each with a
spirit, a piece of god
within, therefore, deserves
to be treated with the same
respect, compassion, and
love, we each hope others
will treat us with as well.

The World We Create

Though life circumstances
influence our path through
life, we each have a choice
how we will live our life.
It matters not whether we are
wealthy or poor; our race,
ethnicity, sex, or any other
differences have little
influence as well.

How we view the world
and live our life is a choice.
Choose to live with
compassion, rather than
indifference, equally
respecting every life,
and selflessly sharing our
love to help all in need.

If we do this, the world
we will discover is one of
beauty, hope, love, and
endless possibilities.

The Beauty of Life

When you look at another,
what do you see?
Do you see their appearance,
flaws, or do you see the pure
beauty of their soul within?

Every person, regardless of
our differences, is perfect.
Discard their outer layer,
the façade we see, to
view the genuine beauty
that has always been
present within each.

Why Are We Angry?

The spirit, present within
every life, knows only
love; negative emotions
do not exist here.
Anger, as are all other
harmful emotions, are
learned as we are indoctrinated
into the world to accept the
self-centered beliefs and
values of the culture
we are raised in.

To rid ourselves of
negative emotions,
embrace the spiritual
path by selflessly
sharing our spirit's
wisdom and unconditional
love with all others.

Doing so will not only
purge these harmful
reactions, but will also
allow us to begin on a
path to find true meaning
in our life as well.

Every Life is Equally Valuable

We are alive to selflessly
share our innate wisdom
and unconditional love,
our spirit, with all others.
It matters not beliefs,
appearance, wealth, genus,
or any other comparisons
we may make.

Every life, regardless of our
differences, is connected,
intimately linked together
by the spirit, a piece of
god present within each.
Each life, therefore,
is equally valuable.

Only when humanity truly
embraces this belief, realizing
the self-centered matrix we are
living in is an illusion, may
the spiritual evolution of
our planet finally begin.

Our Power Within

Within each person an
infinite force exists able
to transform the world.
Though it is often hidden
behind the illusions we
were encouraged to
accept, it remains waiting
patiently for us to free
it from its captivity.

To do so will take great
courage and pain, as we
must confront the many
untruths we accepted as
real when we were
socialized to accept the
beliefs and self-centered
customs of the world.

Those able to do so,
understanding little of
what we learned was
true, will be able to
embrace the unlimited
wisdom and unconditional
love of our spirit within.

With this embrace, we

will unleash our genuine
inherent power, present
within each of us,
allowing us to not
only discover meaning
in our own lives, but to
help transform the world
by sharing our spirit's
wisdom and love, our
power, to help others
realize this as well.

We Have Never Been Alone

Many are lonely, desire
companionship and love,
believing they are alone;
they never have been.
For within every life is
a spirit, a piece of god
accompanying each
of us through life.

When we awaken, we
begin to sense its presence.
With enlightenment, we
fully join with its essence,
understanding our spirit's
eternal presence, and the
intimate connection it
has with all others.

Our Symbiotic Relationship

Sense the beauty, aroma
of nature, of every life
intimately connected to
each other, existing on
our extraordinary planet.
See the radiance, their aura,
vibrate from their core, as
each life networks, coming
alive in their interactions.

Every part of our planet,
every life on it, has a
symbiotic relationship
with each other.
The loss of one, no
matter how insignificant,
effects all.
Only together, acknowledging
the importance and equal
right of each to exist,
may our world spiritually
evolve, mitigating many
of the innumerable
challenges humanity
has created for itself.

Friendship

Friendship is opening
your heart to another, a
stranger even, without intent.
Every life has a universal
purpose: to discover our
mutual spirit, present
within each, then share
it to benefit all.

Spirit represents pure love,
untouched by humanity's
self-centered definition,
meant unite us as one.
With this understanding,
we will realize there
are no strangers.

We are all friends, alive
to selflessly share our
spirit's inherent wisdom
and unconditional love,
reminding each to accept
all others as friends as well.

Our Light

Untethered by man's
interference, the intensity
of the light, present
within each, is blinding.
Its luminous rays penetrate
everything it touches, leaving
pure love in its wake.

With our birth though, our
light begins to dim as we
learn and accept the beliefs
of the self-centered world
in which we are to live.

We then may spend the
rest of our life, trying to
rediscover the vibrant
intensity of our light,
our infinite ability to
share our love, our light,
with the world once more.

A Moment in Time

Our life may change instantly.
If we open our heart, listen
to the silence in between our
racing thoughts, and embrace
the soft tender messages
emanating from our core,
we may awaken to the
genuine possibilities
life truly offers.

By selflessly sharing
the innate wisdom and
unconditional loving
messages we sense, at
that very moment, our
self-centered views,
beliefs, and prejudices
will begin to dissipate,
as we begin on an
enduring journey to
discover our life's
true purpose.

Everyone Has Value

We each will have many
challenges during our lives
that influence the path,
actions, and direction,
our life will take.
For some, the struggles
they face may be
overwhelming, as they
battle the harsh
realities life present.

Despite our differences
or circumstances in life
though, every person
has value and must
not be abandoned.
Though it may be
difficult to be near
someone we consider
unworthy of our time or
friendship, we each
may help change the
direction of another
by selflessly sharing
our love, our spirit
with them, intimately
linking us together.

This one simple act
can change the direction
of their life forever, as
it may trigger them to
awaken, beginning
them on a journey
to remember their
original purpose in life.

We Each May Change the World

We must not wait,
rely on another to
act, magically hoping
life will improve for
those who are struggling,
suffering from living
in an indifferent self-
centered world.

Every person, no matter
our differences or lack of
resources, may change
the direction of the world.
To do so, open your heart,
then selflessly share the
wisdom and infinite love
waiting your permission
to be released.

We Each Must Rely on Another

Every life, regardless
of our differences,
accomplishments, or
genus, is an important
meaningful part of the world.
Since humanity is the dominant
lifeform, they believe they have
the right to cause grievous
harm to other forms of life,
each other, and the planet
that sustains us all.

This self-centered belief is the
underlying cause for many of
humanity's needless problems,
hardships, and challenges.
In truth, every life, is equally
vital, part of an ecosystem
in which we each must
rely on the other.

Senseless injury to
one life, injures all.
Until humanity genuinely
realizes this, the continuing
damage they have and will
continue to do to our planet
and all who live on it,
may prove irreparable.

Before We Can Fix the World

There are many
challenges in the world.
Though some problems
we cannot fix, there
are many others
created by humanity.
War, hunger, prejudice,
inequity, are just a few of
the man-made difficulties
and harmful emotions
affecting countless every day.

There are some who have
tried, frequently in vain,
to alleviate the
struggles of others.
Unfortunately, these
solutions are often temporary,
not fixing the underlying
cause, the self-centered
world in which we live.

Before we may fix the
world and truly help others,
we must first change
ourselves, by embracing
and accepting the inherent
wisdom and messages

of unconditional love
within, then selflessly
sharing those messages,
without motive or
benefit, with all others.
Only then, may our world
finally evolve, assuring a
future for every life
and our planet itself.

The End

Though our mortal body
has a beginning and finite
end, our spirit, a piece
of god accompanying
every life, is immortal.
With death, our physical
body withers as its remains
are cremated or buried.

Our essence, however, who
we truly were when alive,
moves to a higher vibrational
plane, where it joins others,
until called upon once more,
to join another sentient life.

A small part of our
essence, however, also
continues to exist in the
hearts and soul of all
those it influenced
during its last incarnation.
Every interaction we
have, when joined with
a sentient life, regardless
how brief, may influence
the direction of countless others.

Though our body will perish, our essence will continue to live forever in all those we met and inspired during our brief sojourn through life.

Author's Note:

It is my hope your understanding of awakening, enlightenment, and spirituality has been enhanced by reading book 2 of *'Spiritual Reflections'*. If it has, could you please take a few minutes to: "Write a Review" and recommend this book on social media and to your friends and family.

'Spiritual Reflections' was written to try to awaken and help others who are awakened more fully understand what enlightenment is, so their spiritual journey through life may be more fully realized.

Thank you for taking the time to read:

'Spiritual Reflections' – Book 2. Please consider reading the other book in this series as well.

Books by Ken Luball

The four Spiritual books in *The Awakening Tetralogy*:
Today I Am Going to Die: Choices in Life
The Spirit Guide: Journey Through Life
Tranquility: A Village of Hope
The Illusion of Happiness: Choosing Love Over Fear

A Mystical Trilogy. '*Our Search for Meaning*' - a series of three books of thoughtful easily understandable spiritual reflections about awakening, enlightenment, spirituality, & the meaning of life.

A Spiritual Duology: '*Spiritual Reflections*' - Two books of spiritual reflections using metaphor, imagery, and spiritual insight to explore themes of awakening, enlightenment, and the human pursuit of meaning.

****

The first three stories in *The Awakening Tetralogy* are written in the first person, following the spiritual journey through life of a child, as they learn the lessons needed during their life to awaken and become enlightened. These books are written in an understandable, interesting, unique narrative, which is both thought-provoking and engaging.

To find links for each of these nine books please visit my website: kenluball.com.

About Ken

Peace, Love, & Light

∙∙∙

My name is Ken Luball ~ Spiritual ~ Seeker ~ Author ~ Guide

****

Ever since I was a young child, I knew my purpose in life; it was for me to awaken, find enlightenment, and share my experience and knowledge with others. To reach those lofty aspirations though, I first had to navigate through quite a few unexpected detours in my life. Though I was brought up in a religious family, it did not help me hear the messages from my spirit guide, Bodhi. If anything, religion only further isolated me, teaching me to accept the ego's view of religion rather than Bodhi's. It was not until after I stopped following a formal religion, I finally was able to embrace spirituality, and with this embrace, I awoke.

Spirituality is the belief there is a piece of god, a spirit, within everything that has life, and, because of this, all life is important, equal, and connected. After I awoke, no longer having the dogma of religion handicapping my views, I was suddenly free to explore this philosophy of life more deeply. Only then did I become aware of the mask I wore and the impenetrable wall I had erected around my heart; the mask and wall allowed me to survive in the world. I would always smile, appear happy, though I would often feel intense anxiety within. This was something I never really understood until the moment I confronted my ego. Little did I know these survival mechanisms would have a profound effect on me for the majority of my life. By protecting me from emotional pain, they also isolated me from my family, everyone else in my life, and even from myself. No one could hurt me because I did not allow anyone to get close enough to do so. In turn, no one could love me or was I able to truly love another either. This superficial life, one devoid of risk or pain, left me alone in a sea of people.

It took many years before the first cracks in my wall formed and before I could loosen the mask I constantly wore. It took me almost an entire lifetime to awaken and begin my journey toward enlightenment.

After I was clearly able to hear my spirit guide, Bodhi, I realized everything I had learned from my ego throughout my life was untrue. I had looked for love and happiness in the job I had, the money I made, things I owned, and through my wife and children. With the exception of the latter, I finally realized none of those things truly mattered. This does not mean I am ungrateful to my ego, however. It taught me coping skills and allowed me to succeed, or at least what I thought success was. Though my ego still remains with me, it has taken a more secondary role in my life now, relinquishing its former primary role to my spirit guide, Bodhi.

Decisions were now required. While it was tempting to take this newly found state of being, withdraw from society and all the hate, fear, cruelty, poverty, and greed that plagues it, I knew within myself, this knowledge was to be shared with others. That is my destiny. Therefore, I have written 𝔄 𝔐𝔶𝔰𝔱𝔦𝔠𝔞𝔩 𝔗𝔯𝔦𝔩𝔬𝔤𝔶: *'Our Search for Meaning'*: a series of three books of thoughtful easily understandable spiritual reflections about life; 𝔄 𝔖𝔭𝔦𝔯𝔦𝔱𝔲𝔞𝔩 𝔇𝔲𝔬𝔩𝔬𝔤𝔶: *'Spiritual Reflections'*: two books of spiritual reflections using metaphor, imagery, and spiritual insight to explore themes of awakening, enlightenment, and the human pursuit of meaning; and 𝔗𝔥𝔢 𝔄𝔴𝔞𝔨𝔢𝔫𝔦𝔫𝔤 𝔗𝔢𝔱𝔯𝔞𝔩𝔬𝔤𝔶 : the first three stories in *The Awakening Tetralogy* follow the spiritual journey through life of a child, as they learn the lessons needed during their life to awaken and become enlightened. It is my hope you will read these books, and in doing so, begin a new adventure; one where you will awaken and further your journey toward enlightenment with your spirit within.

I do not know if these books will be widely read in my lifetime, though I hope one day they may help others awaken and find enlightenment as well.

"We are all on a spiritual journey of love & peace; together may we spread light throughout the world."

To read more of Ken's life-changing reflections visit his website:
kenluball.com

Appendix: Spiritual Reflections ~ 2

      Glossary……p.3
1) You Are Worthwhile……p.5
2) The First Step to Awakening……p.6
3) This is Enlightenment……p.7
4) Reviewing My Life……p.8
5) Taking Advantage of Others……p.9
6) Light……p.10
7) Remember……p.11
8) A Universal Tenet……p.12
9) The World We See……p.13
10) The Universe……p.14
11) Meaning……p.15
12) The Waterfall……p.16
13) Givers and Takers……p.17
14) We Are Stronger Together……p.18
15) The Ceiling……p.19
16) Our False Beliefs……p.20
17) We Are All Children of the World……p.21
18) The Bird……p.22
19) The Sun……p.24
20) Listen……p.26
21) See Beyond……p.27

22) Finding Meaning......p.28
23) Our Common Purpose?......p.29
24) The Beauty of Life......p.30
25) Tears......p.31
26) The Power of Love......p.32
27) The Aurora......p.33
28) A Moment of Sanity......p.34
29) After We Awaken......p.35
30) Our Search for Meaning......p.37
31) The Paradox of Life......p.38
32) Our Most Important Designation......p.39
33) Life's Genuine Value......p.40
34) Our Ego's Motives......p.41
35) Our Spirit Will Endure......p.42
36) This is How Enlightened Soul Sees the World......p.43
37) Only Together May We All Flourish......p.44
38) Our Innate Wisdom......p.45
39) The Sky......p.46
40) We Are One Spirit......p.47
41) Two Choices......p.48
42) Only Together May We Find Meaning......p.49
43) Our Spirit Lives Forever......p.50
44) What is Success?......p.51
45) Our Beliefs......p.52

46) We Are One People……p.53
47) Every Life is Important……p.54
48) When We See Another……p.55
49) Absolute Love……p.56
50) Light or Darkness……p.57
51) We Must Help Each Other……p.58
52) Helping Others Tirelessly……p.59
53) Why Are We Alive?……p.60
54) The Reason for Our Existence……p.61
55) The Good in Others……p.62
56) What Do You See?……p.63
57) The Reason We Are Alive……p.64
58) The Path to Enlightenment……p.65
59) A Well Lived Life……p.66
60) How We View Life……p.67
61) See Only the Good……p.68
62) The Genuine Purpose of Life……p.69
63) Our Desired Destination……p.70
64) The Realization……p.71
65) The Guru……p.72
66) The Problem With the Ego……p.73
67) As Death Approaches……p.74
68) Living Life in Fear or Love……p.75
69) Spiritual Debt……p.76
70) Why Are We Alive?……p.77

71) Treat Others With Kindness……p.78

72) The Genuine Reason for Our Life's Journey……p.79

73) Humanity's Indifference……p.80

74) Undoing the Damage……p.81

75) Taking Advantage of Others……p.82

76) Living in a Split Reality……p.83

77) The Healers……p.85

78) Why Are We Alive?……p.86

79) Our Primary Decision Maker……p.87

80) Needless Death……p.88

81) Life's Genuine Intentions……p.89

82) Our Focus in Life……p.90

83) The World of Enlightenment……p.91

84) The Journey Back……p.92

85) What is Normal?……p.94

86) We're So Vain……p.95

87) Spiritual Love……p.97

88) The Message……p.98

89) See Beyond Our Differences……p.99

90) Love Unites Us……p.100

91) Together……p.101

92) I Am God……p.102

93) Judging Others……p.103

94) Our Spirit Will Live On……p.104

95)	The Matrix We Created……p.105	
96)	Why is There?……p.106	
97)	Helping Each Other……p.107	
98)	Look Past the Pain……p.108	
99)	A World of Kindness, Empathy. & Love……p.109	
100)	Finding Love and Happiness……p.110	
101)	Every Life is Equally Valuable……p.111	
102)	The Truth……p.112	
103)	You Are Beautiful……p.113	
104)	I Love You……p.114	
105)	Open Your Eyes……p.115	
106)	Living Without Fear……p.116	
107)	I Am Your Spirit……p.117	
108)	Our Untapped Potential……p.119	
109)	Our Value……p.120	
110)	Our Children are Watching……p.121	
111)	I Was Blind, But Now I See……p.123	
112)	Blaming Others……p.124	
113)	Labels……p.125	
114)	Living in a World of Love……p.127	
115)	How Many More?……p.128	
116)	Freedom……p.129	
117)	The Reason for Life……p.130	
118)	Caring About Each Other……p.131	

119) Life's Genuine Purpose……p.132
120) What is Our Value?……p.133
121) Is One Life More Important Than Another?……p.134
122) Be A Good Person……p.135
123) A World of Hope……p.136
124) A Sensitive Heart……p.137
125) Tribalism……p.138
126) The Entitled……p.139
127) Sharing Your Authentic-Self……p.140
128) What is Enlightenment?……p.141
129) One Belief……p.142
130) Let It Go……p.143
131) Two Realities……p.144
132) Our Human Self (Ego)……p.146
133) The Glass……p.147
134) Our Angry Planet……p.149
135) Ocoee……p.150
136) The Lighthouse……p.151
137) Our Soul……p.152
138) Our Divisions……p.153
139) The Victim……p.155
140) The Complainer……p.156
141) Judging Others……p.157
142) Poison……p.158

143) Who Are We?......p.160
144) We Are All Family......p.161
145) The Right to Exist......p.162
146) Our Genuine Power......p.163
147) Intolerance......p.164
148) Honor Everyone......p.165
149) Spiritual Philosophy......p.166
150) The Eclipse......p.168
151) Another Choice......p.169
152) The Distraction......p.170
153) Dying of the Light......p.171
154) The Spirit Within......p.172
155) Inequality......p.173
156) Controlling Our Ego......p.174
157) Why Are We Born?......p.176
158) What is Truth?......p.177
159) The Fog of Life......p.179
160) Our Aura......p.181
161) The Balcony......p.182
162) Priorities......p.183
163) Happiness......p.184
164) Darkness and Light......p.185
165) Our Journey Through Life......p.187
166) Human vs Spiritual Plane......p.189
167) The Virus......p.191

168) The Cost of Enlightenment……p.192
169) How Long?……p.194
170) The Eyes of a Child……p.195
171) A Glimmer of Light……p.197
172) Follow Your Heart……p.199
173) Walk With Humility……p.200
174) Listen……p.201
175) It's All Noise……p.202
176) Our Internal Struggle……p.203
177) Our Harmful Emotions……p.204
178) The Source……p.205
179) Captives in Life……p.206
180) Accept the Message You Hear……p.207
181) This is Enlightenment……p.208
182) The Darkness Behind Our Smile……p.209
183) Apathy……p.211
184) Death……p.212
185) From Pain to Wisdom……p.213
186) Our Words……p.214
187) Helping All in Need……p.215
188) We Are Children of the World……p.217
189) Every Life is Sentient……p.218
190) The Cure……p.219
191) Judging Each Other……p.220
192) Compassion, Love, and Humanity……p.222

193)	The Lessons We Are Born to Learn……p.223	
194)	Forgiveness……p.224	
195)	Why Are We Born?……p.225	
196)	How Do You Know You Are Awake?……p.226	
197)	Trusting Each Other……p.227	
198)	We Are All Related……p.228	
199)	Our Children May Change the World……p.229	
200)	We Must Not Remain Apathetic……p.230	
201)	Life……p.231	
202)	The Truth Translator……p.232	
203)	The Price of Life……p.233	
204)	The Ostrich……p.235	
205)	We Must Not Fail……p.237	
206)	One Truth……p.238	
207)	Power……p.239	
208)	Echoes in Life……p.240	
209)	Every Life is Valuable……p.241	
210)	A Human Issue……p.242	
211)	We Are All Brothers and Sisters……p.244	
212)	The Essence of Life……p.246	
213)	Human Capacity……p.247	
214)	In Darkness, See the Light……p.249	
215)	Our Essence……p.251	
216)	Mental Illness……p.252	
217)	Our Self……p.254	

218) We Are One People……p.256
219) The Battle for Supremacy……p.257
220) What Really Matters?……p.258
221) How Can I Help?……p.259
222) The Evolution of Humanity……p.260
223) An Alternate Reality……p.262
224) The First Step to Awakening……p.263
225) A New Beginning……p.264
226) Life's True Purpose……p.266
227) Money or Meaning……p.267
228) Why Are We Alive?……p.268
229) Success……p.269
230) We Are Alive to Help Each Other……p.270
231) Life's Genuine Purpose……p.271
232) The Deep State……p.272
233) A Moment of Grace……p.273
234) The Negotiator……p.274
235) Inequality……p.276
236) The World We Create……p.277
237) The Beauty of Life……p.278
238) Why Are We Angry?……p.279
239) Every Life is Equally Valuable……p.280
240) Our Power Within……p.281
241) We Have Never Been Alone……p.283
242) Our Symbiotic Relationship……p.284

243) Friendship......p.285
244) Our Light......p.286
245) A Moment in Time......p.287
246) Everyone Has Value......p.288
247) We Each May Change the World......p.290
248) We Each Must Rely on Another......p.291
249) Before We Can Fix the World......p.292
250) The End......p.294

"Why are we alive?" This timeless question lies at the heart of *'Spiritual Reflections' – Book 2*. Written in clear, easily understandable language, these additional 250 spiritual reflections use metaphor, imagery, and spiritual insight to explore themes of awakening, enlightenment, and the human pursuit of meaning, as it guides readers toward a deeper understanding of life's true purpose.

Ken Luball ~ Spiritual ~ Seeker ~ Author ~ Guide ~

'Our Search for Meaning', a series of 3 books of spiritual reflections. *'Spiritual Reflections'*, 2 books of spiritual insight about awakening, enlightenment, & spirituality and *The Awakening Tetralogy'*, a series of four spiritual novels, were written to try to awaken and help others, who are awakened, more fully understand what enlightenment is, so their journey through life may be more fully realized. Having a lifelong obsession to discover the true meaning of life, Ken is committed to sharing stories, anecdotes, and lessons he has learned to help others further their understanding about their life's genuine purpose as well.

www.ingramcontent.com/pod-product-compliance
Lightning Source LLC
Chambersburg PA
CBHW050523100526
44581CB00002B/88